BLACK&DECKER®

THE COMPLETE GUIDE TO

PORCHES &
PATIO ROOMS

Creative Publishing
international

MINNEAPOLIS, MINNESOTA
www.creativepub.com

Creative Publishing international

Copyright © 2009
Creative Publishing international, Inc.
400 First Avenue North, Suite 300
Minneapolis, Minnesota 55401
1-800-328-0590
www.creativepub.com

Printed in the United States of America

10 9 8 7 6 5 4 3 2

Library of Congress Cataloging-in-Publication Data

The complete guide to porches & patio rooms : sunrooms, patio
enclosures, breezeways & screened porches.
      p. cm.
  At head of title: Black & Decker.
  Includes index.
  Summary: "Offers design advice and easy-to-follow, concise
instructions for adding porches and other outdoor rooms to a
home"--Provided by publisher.
  ISBN-13: 978-1-58923-420-8 (soft cover)
  ISBN-10: 1-58923-420-0 (soft cover)
  1. Porches. 2. Sunspaces. 3. Patios. I. Title: Complete guide to
porches and patio rooms.
  TH3000.S85C66 2009
  690'.893--dc22
                            2008031689

President/CEO: Ken Fund
VP for Sales & Marketing: Kevin Hamric

Home Improvement Group

Publisher: Bryan Trandem
Managing Editor: Tracy Stanley
Senior Editor: Mark Johanson
Editor: Jennifer Gehlhar

Creative Director: Michele Lanci-Altomare
Senior Design Managers: Jon Simpson, Brad Springer
Design Manager: James Kegley

Lead Photographer: Steve Galvin
Photo Coordinator: Joanne Wawra
Shop Manager: Bryan McLain
Shop Assistant: Cesar Fernandez Rodriguez
Shop Help: Charlie Boldt

Production Managers: Linda Halls, Laura Hokkanen

Page Layout Artist: Danielle Smith
Photographers: Andrea Rugg
Author: Philip Schmidt

Cover photo: photography by Brian Vanden Brink;
architectural design by Dominic Mercadante

The Complete Guide to Porches & Patio Rooms
Created by: The Editors of Creative Publishing international, Inc., in cooperation with Black & Decker.
Black & Decker® is a trademark of The Black & Decker Corporation and is used under license.

NOTICE TO READERS

For safety, use caution, care, and good judgment when following the procedures described in this book. The publisher and Black & Decker cannot assume responsibility for any damage to property or injury to persons as a result of misuse of the information provided.

The techniques shown in this book are general techniques for various applications. In some instances, additional techniques not shown in this book may be required. Always follow manufacturers' instructions included with products, since deviating from the directions may void warranties. The projects in this book vary widely as to skill levels required: some may not be appropriate for all do-it-yourselfers, and some may require professional help.

Consult your local building department for information on building permits, codes, and other laws as they apply to your project.

Contents

The Complete Guide to Porches & Patio Rooms

Introduction

Once a standard feature on American homes of all types, the traditional covered porch all but disappeared over the course of the 20th century. Until recently, this unique indoor-outdoor room and many of its everyday benefits seemed lost to a bygone era. But today the porch is making a comeback in a big way as homeowners are rediscovering the simple pleasures of a sheltered space that's just a step from the main house but can feel like a world apart—casual, communal, welcoming, and, best of all, full of fresh air and sunlight. Not coincidentally, sunrooms, three-season porches, and other patio rooms are now more popular than ever and are joining porches at the top of homeowners' wish lists.

So why did we disregard the porch in the first place? Several factors have been suggested: a shift in architectural tastes, economies in home building, or perhaps a subtle decline in community interaction, among others. In many regions the biggest change came with the advent of air conditioning; with indoor comfort achieved by flicking a switch, there was no need to rely on nature for relief from summer's heat. As the porch began to lose favor, it was increasingly replaced by backyard patios and elevated decks. But while these do an adequate job of encouraging us to get outdoors, they have a decidedly different feel, and more limited uses, than a porch or patio room.

Unlike decks and open patios, which lack overhead shelter, porches and enclosed patios can be enjoyed during rainstorms and when the sun is bearing down at midday. (In fact, a summer rain shower is one of the best excuses to linger on a porch.) A three-season porch, with its plentiful windows that are easily opened or closed depending on the weather, is the perfect stage for watching the seasons change. And a sunroom can be a delightful retreat no matter what's happening outside. The additional shelter of a porch or patio room also allows for more flexibility with furnishing and decorating the space, even if that means nothing more than a rocking chair and a soft light for reading by after the sun goes down.

If you're thinking about adding a new porch or sunroom, or maybe converting an ordinary patio into a more versatile indoor-outdoor space, this book can guide you through every phase of the project. The Portfolio section is there to inspire ideas with its photographic gallery of beautiful outdoor rooms. The two sections that follow take you right into the planning and construction details, helping you to narrow your focus and refine your plans. From there, any of the dozens of step-by-step projects will show you how to get the job done, whether you're doing the work yourself or hiring it out to professionals.

Portfolio of Porches & Patio Rooms

When design professionals begin the planning stages on a new project, they often ask their clients to provide examples of things they like, usually in the form of magazine clippings, dog-eared book pages, photographs of neighbors' houses—anything that captures an emotion or conveys an idea. The designer's goal is not to borrow concepts or fast-track the brainstorming process; it is to help the clients discover what they really want by first exploring the possibilities. In this section of the book, you're invited to take an inspirational, and occasionally practical, look at some of the many, many things you can do with a new porch or patio room.

Of course, choosing the major elements that will shape the plan of your project—the size, layout, construction, finishes, and overall look—are big decisions. But even more important is blending just the right elements to achieve the special emotional quality you desire. A porch or patio room is meant to be a personal space. Your space. Take the time to imagine yourself enjoying the room on a daily basis. This is the key to creating a truly cherished, well-used part of your home—something that is much more than an attractive addition.

In this chapter:

- Open Porches
- Enclosed Porches & Patios
- Sunrooms

Open Porches

If you've ever lived in a house with a *bona fide* porch, you probably already know why people love them so much. While decks and patios are great for grilling steaks or basking in the sun, there's nothing quite like the feel of relaxing on a good porch. Wide open to the breezes, yet sheltered from the rain and hottest sun, a traditional porch is the perfect blend of indoor and outdoor space—a magical combination that somehow conveys the very essence of leisure.

Of course, a porch doesn't have to be made of wood or even be wide open to *feel* like a porch. Porches come in all shapes and sizes. Some are fancy, some rustic. Some offer private seclusion, while others invite neighbors to stop by for a chat. But regardless of its size, style, or location, a porch lets you get out

of the house without having to leave home. Deciding what you'll *do* when you get out there—that is, how (and when) you'll use the porch most often, should become the guiding principle for all of the planning that follows.

If you're also hoping to improve the look of your home, keep in mind that a well-designed porch can perform architectural wonders. It can make a bland facade picturesque or turn an uninviting front door into a gracious, welcoming entrance. It can even enhance the overall decorative scheme, lending legitimacy to existing but perhaps ineffectual details. In short, a porch adds curb appeal like no other embellishment can. So, what could a porch do for you?

What could be more inviting to family and friends than a lineup of rocking chairs and an open view to your little piece of the world unfolding before you?

A traditional porch swing adds a quintessential touch to this turn-of-the-century open porch. The swing serves as both a boundary and an invitation to relax in the shade.

Simple yet nicely proportioned, this porch with hipped roof fits perfectly against the backdrop of the home's gable-end wall.

Open railings are ideal for defining a porch's boundaries without closing off the space. Hanging plants and flowerpots are another way to blend decoration with a subtle sense of enclosure.

A good porch needs to satisfy only what the house and its owners call for. This house desperately needed shelter for its entry door. The owners wisely expanded the roof design to incorporate the window and provided just enough room for a sitting area.

A large open porch is perfect on farm-house style homes, where it both shelters the entryway and creates a comfortable sitting area. In some climates and regions, however, insects can make an open porch less practical.

For those who love a garden environment, a little weathering, mature vines, and plenty of seasonal plants and flowers are essential ingredients.

Here is a good example of what a porch can do for a flat front facade. Old homes like this lose a great deal of character when their original porches are neglected and, ultimately, removed.

The clean lines and stately flavor of this newer home set the tone for its open front porch. Separating the porch roof from the entryway gives the space prominence and enhances the "outdoor room" effect.

A portico—traditionally a small, projecting roof supported by columns over an entryway—isn't exactly a porch, but this can be a great feature for adding definition to an entry and providing shelter for visitors at the front door.

Upgrades to this older porch included poured concrete steps and painted iron railings, creating a nice contrast with the original wood construction materials.

Two approaches to an approach: At left, a tapering staircase and an opening centered on the front door say "welcome" loud and clear. At right, while no less inviting, an extra turn to the front door focuses more attention on the porch itself and builds anticipation for reaching the final destination.

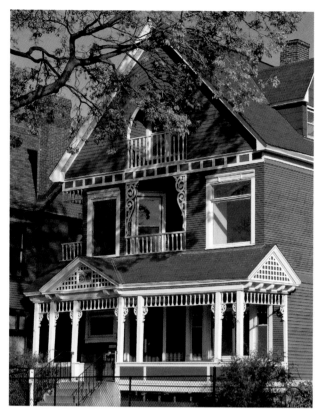

Faithful architectural detailing is critical to designing porches for period homes. To make the porch fit in, it's important to complement the home's rooflines, trim, and other decorative elements.

A breezeway is a unique building feature joining two structures with a porch-like roof. Linking a house entry with a detached garage or carriage house, for example, a breezeway offers a great opportunity to turn a transition space into a homey porch setting.

This classic-looking front porch has a distinctive feature that sets it apart from most standard designs: The gable end on the shed roof frames the top of an eye-catching composition including the columns, steps, and side railings, all centered over the front door.

Enclosed Porches & Patios

Screened-in porches and patios represent the next level in indoor-outdoor living. For many, this is the best of both worlds: a warm, sun-sheltered spot for enjoying fresh air and the sights and sounds of the surrounding landscape—all without the considerable nuisance of bugs. Going a step further by filling the wall openings with windows provides additional shelter against rain and uncomfortably cool breezes and can extend the usable time of the room well into the transitional seasons. But if you're trying to decide between all screens and all windows, the answer, not surprisingly, depends on how you plan to use the room.

Screened rooms are for warm weather, period. Most of them simply don't get used in the cooler days of spring and fall, and yet, that's a big part of why they're so special. Screened rooms are made for that all-too-short summer season of outdoor entertaining, afternoon naps in the shade, and long, lazy evenings when it's just too nice or too hot to be indoors. When the temperature begins to drop, the beloved room sits empty, a summer memory, until it's rediscovered as a favorite hangout the following spring.

Glassed-in porches and patios, or three-season rooms, are designed for use in every season except winter, when their uninsulated walls and windows make the rooms impractical to heat in colder climates. Three-season rooms are often ideal in spring and fall, and any time when it's just a little too cold to be outside. The rooms' plentiful windows allow their interiors to be warmed by the sun without the chilling effect of airflow. In summer, maximum ventilation is important, as even open windows can prove too restrictive during the hottest days.

Anyone who lives at a higher elevation is used to dramatic swings in daily temperatures. An enclosed outdoor room is great for buffering those chilly mornings, blazing-hot noontimes, and pleasant sunsets that quickly turn cold.

Glassed-in patios serve adequately as three-season porches in almost every climate and can be used all year in mild climates. Large operating windows are essential for providing ventilation in warm weather.

In this well-appointed screened porch, the furnishings tell the story. A wicker sofa, a coffee table, and an end table with a lamp suggest a casual twist on a formal living room setting, while the porch swing is all about outdoor leisure.

At the opposite end of the spectrum from a screened room, an enclosed porch can have conventionally framed and finished walls and look like an ordinary addition from the exterior.

Desiring a truly built-in look, these homeowners opted for full-height brick wing walls and a short kneewall to anchor their enclosed porch addition to their home.

This beautiful sun porch is clearly an add-on, but its proportions and detailing complement the house perfectly.

Adjacent to the home's living and dining rooms, this expansive screened patio is seamlessly linked to the interior with large glass doors.

The best of both worlds: The insulated bump-out to the right serves as a year-round sunroom for this home, while the adjacent screened patio is a haven for warm weather.

Large slider windows and lean structural elements help preserve a simple, outdoor feel on this backyard deck converted to a three-season porch.

Wraparound porches can be ideal for adding a screened or three-season room, providing plenty of space for an enclosure and an open porch.

Because this wraparound enclosed porch makes up the first story of the home's facade, it needed to look like part of the original design. Prominent, trimmed columns and substantial, symmetrically arranged framing members on the screened openings give the porch a structural quality that visually supports the rest of the house.

A fireplace on a screened porch? Why not? Just as with an indoor fireplace, an outdoor hearth creates the perfect setting for gathering and socializing on cool evenings.

Kneewalls add privacy and a greater sense of enclosure. Here, the low walls create a cozy backdrop for furniture and add just the right formal touch for an outdoor dining room.

Sunrooms

For anyone who feels pangs of envy whenever they see a cat curled up in a pool of sunlight under a window, a sunroom is just the thing. By any definition, a sunroom is an interior space with lots and lots of windows, with the express purpose of bringing in lots and lots of sunlight. Designed for year-round use in any climate, a sunroom is a home's very own shrine to the sun, a constant invitation to come in and make like a cat.

The chief distinction between sunrooms and three-season porches is that sunrooms are completely insulated—including the floor, walls, roof, and windows—so that the space can be heated and cooled like any indoor room. This also means a sunroom is integrated with the rest of the house and works more like a room addition than an indoor-outdoor space. While a sunroom may not have the same outdoor feel that a porch has, its many windows can provide open views to the outdoors. This visual connection can be greatly enhanced when the sunroom projects beyond the main footprint of the house.

Sunrooms come in all shapes and sizes and may be known by several different names, but most fall into one of a few broad categories. A classic sunroom is a three-sided affair that juts out from a main house wall and has a framed roof that may be solid or glazed. A conservatory is a glassed-in room with lean framing and, typically, a glazed roof. Originally designed for cultivating fruit trees and other warm-weather plants in colder climates (primarily Britain), conservatories seem as much like greenhouses as conventional rooms. Finally, a solarium is a framed glass lean-to structure attached to a house, often with a continuous curve joining the wall and roof sections.

Some sunroom kits are lightweight enough to go right on top of an existing deck. Depending on the climate, this type of room can be great for three-season or year-round use.

Elegant and airy, this sunroom is clearly decorated for a summery feel. White is always a good choice in a sunroom: It reflects light nicely and helps minimize heat gain, and it de-emphasizes window frames and other obstructions to the view.

Solarium-style sunrooms often take the form of a bump-out to an existing interior room. It's like a room-sized garden window for you and your plants.

To help minimize the darkening effect of its solid roof, this modern sunroom has fully glazed, heightened walls. A glass interior door with surrounding windows brings ample light into the adjacent room.

Tucked in between (what were) two exterior walls, this cozy sunspace has become an intimate living and entertaining room that feels miles away from the TV room and other everyday hangouts.

A three- or four-sided conservatory is the ultimate sunroom. However, a completely glazed room like this isn't practical for every climate; hot summer sun can be difficult to contend with.

Positioned for maximum sun exposure during the cooler months of the year, this sunroom kit includes heat-blocking ceiling shades for added comfort in the summer.

With the leanest possible framing—painted green—and nothing but glass elsewhere, this magical conservatory seems as much a part of the landscape as the vines clinging to its walls.

Fully screened openings provide ample ventilation for this convertible sunroom, while the glazed ceiling panels permit light and protect the rear entry from rain showers.

Appropriate for almost any style of home, French doors are ideally suited to sunrooms. They let in loads of light and air and can be opened wide for easy passage into the house or out to the yard.

Manufactured and kit sunrooms can be installed for much less than custom additions and with little or no alteration of the house or outdoor elements. Here, the sunroom kit sits atop a new wood deck built on the ground. The kit included its own door for convenient outdoor access.

A "patio suite" is probably a better term than "patio room" to describe this extravagant indoor/outdoor living area. Clear polycarbonate panels are employed to close off the roof surrounding the gazebo as well as to create see-through sidewalls. The patterned porcelain floor tile ties the rooms together visually.

While this spectacular custom sunroom is out of reach for most people's budget, its traditional details and symmetrical design can be inspiring for anyone seeking a refined, formal aesthetic. Note how the solid, frame-and-panel corner sections balance the weight of the heavy cornice and create a nice contrast to the fine glazing bars on the large windows.

Solid kneewalls are common features for both custom and manufactured sunrooms and conservatories. Cladding the low walls with the same finish that's on the exterior house walls is an effective way to ensure architectural continuity.

Detached from the house, a sunroom becomes a summerhouse, a magical retreat for lazy afternoons or a shining centerpiece for outdoor parties.

Building Porches & Patio Rooms

This section will guide you through the steps of building a porch or enclosing a patio from the ground up. First, you'll see how to transform a minimal front entry into an attractive open porch with a framed floor and roof. From there, you'll learn how to add railings, build new wood or concrete steps, and even screen-in the porch using any of a number of popular techniques. Next comes a detailed project for building a complete three-season porch addition. Enclosing a porch can be much like building a porch, with a few key differences. Two custom patio enclosures are shown here, along with a quick and easy method for claiming under-deck space for a new patio room. Because of the similarities in construction, you might choose to adapt design elements from the porch projects to use in a patio enclosure, or vice versa.

In this chapter:

- Planning a Porch or Patio Project
- Front Porches
- Porch Railings
- Wood Porch Steps
- Concrete Steps
- Portico
- Screened-in Porches
- Underdeck Enclosure
- Enclosure Screen Kit
- Screen Doors
- Patio Shelter
- Patio Enclosures
- Patio Arbor/Trellis Enclosure
- Three-Season Porch

Planning a Porch or Patio Project

The adage "form follows function" applies as much to a porch or patio project as it does to any other architectural design. Begin your planning by listing ways you would like to use your new porch or patio. Are you looking mainly for a comfortable spot where you can contemplate your garden in summer bloom, or do you want a light-filled place where you can enjoy your coffee and the morning paper throughout most of the year?

Next, take stock of your property. Is there room to build around your existing landscape elements without major removal or additions? Is the proposed area exposed to direct sunlight or high winds? Sketching a site drawing will help you assess these factors. Also consider the style and construction of your house. If you are thinking about adding a porch, for example, would it look best with a peaked gable roof that matches your house roof, or would a flat roof blend in better? Once you have made some initial decisions about the project that is best for you, enlist the aid of an architect or a designer. He or she can help you develop ideas into detailed design drawings needed to obtain a building permit. Also consult your local building department. The inspectors there can supply you with information about building codes and other requirements that will affect your project.

This section shows:

- Designing Your Project
- Working with Inspectors & Building Codes
- Working Safely
- Basic Hand Tools

Consult a design professional to help you create a detailed construction plan for your project. Unless you have a great deal of experience with frame carpentry and house construction, you should have a professionally drawn plan before starting any major project, like adding a porch or a patio enclosure.

Designing Your Project

Evaluate the planned project site: Note locations of windows, electrical service lines, and any other obstructions that might affect the positioning or design of a porch or a patio structure. For example, if you are interested in building a front porch, note the distance from the front door to any nearby windows; any design you come up with must be large enough to include the window, or small enough to stop short of it. Also assess the building materials used in and around the planned project area. For example, the yellow stucco walls on the house at right would be a natural fit with any clay-based or earth-colored building materials, like terra-cotta patio tile.

Consider the roofline of your house for projects that are attached to the house and include their own roof. The house to the left had just enough second-floor exterior wall space that a porch could be attached to it without the need for tying the porch roof directly to the roof of the house—a project for professionals only. The patio enclosure at the right takes advantage of the low, flat roof on the house expansion by extending the roofline to meet the sunroom roof.

(continued)

Measure your proposed project area, then draw a scale plan on which you can sketch ideas. Your plan should include relevant features, such as shade patterns, trees, and other landscaping details. Also measure the height of door thresholds and the length and height of any walls or buildings adjacent to the proposed project area.

Measure the slope of the proposed building site to determine if you would need to do any grading work. Drive stakes at each end of the area, then tie a mason's string between the stakes. Use a line level to set the string to level. At each stake, measure from the string to the ground. The difference in the distances, when calculated over the distance between the stakes, will give you the slope. If the slope is greater than 1" per foot, you may need to regrade the building site. Consult a landscape architect.

Measure the roof slope of your house, and try to use the same slope if the project you are planning includes a roof. Hold a carpenter's square against the roofline with the long arm perfectly horizontal. Position the square so the long arm intersects the roof at the 12" mark. On the short arm, measure down to the point of intersection. The number of inches will give you the roof slope in a 12" span. For example, if the top of the square is 4" from the roofline, then your roof slope is 4-in-12.

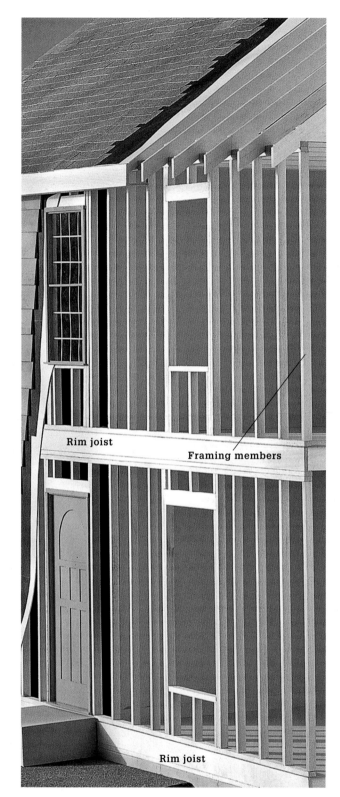

Identify your siding type: Stucco: If you have stucco siding, plan on a fair amount of work if your project requires you to remove siding, as when installing a ledger board. To remove the stucco siding, first score the outline of the area to be removed with a chisel. Next, cut the stucco using a circular saw with a masonry blade. Make multiple passes, increasing the blade depth by ⅛" increments until the blade reaches the stucco lath. Chisel the stucco away inside the cut-out area using a cold chisel, and cut out the lath with aviator snips.

Learn about house construction. The model above shows the basic construction of a platform-framed house—by far the most common type of framing today. Pay special attention to locations of rim joists and framing members, since you likely will need to anchor any large porch or patio project to one or both of these elements.

Lap siding: Whether it is wood, aluminum, or vinyl, lap siding is much easier to remove than stucco, and it should not be considered an impediment when planning a project. To remove it, simply set the blade of a circular saw to a cutting depth equal to the siding thickness (usually about ¾"), and make straight cuts at the edges of the removal area. Finish the cuts at the corners with a chisel, and remove the siding.

Working with Inspectors & Building Codes

Any addition made to your house must comply with local zoning ordinances and building codes that specify where and how you can build.

In most areas, building codes are created by the building or planning department in your municipal government. These departments are staffed by inspectors, who are trained to answer questions, provide information, grant building permits, and make on-site inspections of some building projects. Get to know your local inspectors at the beginning of your project. View them as a helpful resource for a successful project.

The specific types of projects that require building permits varies between localities, but it is safe to say that any major project, like a new porch or a patio enclosure, will require a permit. To be granted a permit, you must present a detailed plan that includes both an elevation drawing and a floor plan (see page 37). There are some very specific conventions you must follow in creating these drawings, so get assistance if you have not done this kind of work before. You also will be required to pay a permit fee, which likely is based on the projected cost of the project.

In some cases, projects that are designed to occupy space near property borders or municipal sidewalks or streets may require that you get a variance from your local zoning commission. Discuss this possibility with a local inspector.

Mark property lines and measure distances from the planned project area to municipal sidewalks or streets before developing a detailed project plan. To avoid future disputes, mark property lines as though they are 1 ft. closer in than they actually are.

Concrete frost footings are required for many porch and patio projects. The frost line is the first point below ground level where freezing will not occur. Frost lines may be 48" or deeper in colder climates. Always build frost footings 1 ft. past the frost line.

Project Features Affected by Codes ▸

- CONSTRUCTION MATERIALS: Building codes often prescribe minimum sizes for structural members of your project, like deck joists, beams, posts, and ledgers.
- FASTENERS: Screw sizes and spacing are usually indicated for most parts of the project, from structural elements to roof decking.
- TOTAL SIZE: Height, width, and estimated weight of the project must be suitable for the support methods used. Comply with any neighborhood covenants.
- FOOTINGS: Codes define what, if any, footing requirements affect your project (photo, right).

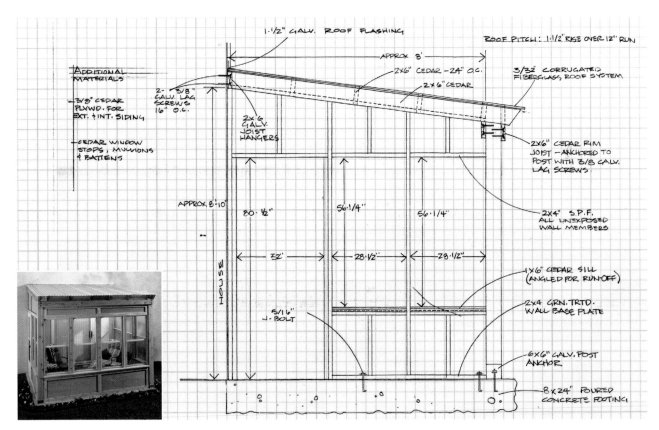

A building section drawing shows sizes and locations of structural elements, such as footing, ledger, studs, beams, rafters, door and window headers, as well as roof pitch and the type of roof covering planned. It also notes specific building materials and fasteners.

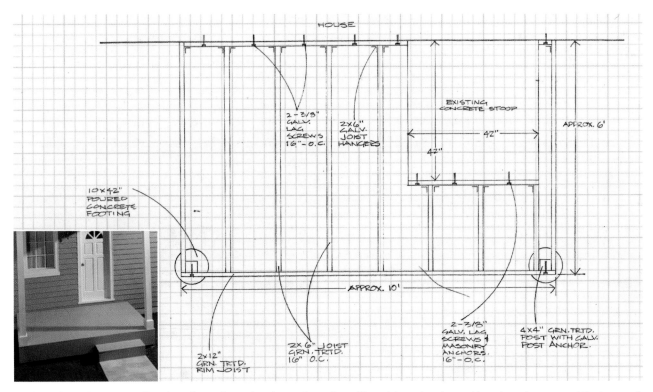

A plan view shows overall project dimensions, the size and spacing of floor joists, the size and location of posts, and the types of hardware to be used for connecting and anchoring structural members.

Working Safely

Working on porches or patios means working outdoors. By taking commonsense precautions you can work just as safely outdoors as indoors, even though the exterior of your house presents a few additional safety considerations.

Building projects for porches and patios frequently require that you use ladders or scaffolding. Learn and follow basic safety rules for working at heights.

Any time you are working outside, the weather conditions should play a key role in just about every aspect of how you conduct your work—from the clothes you wear to the amount of work you decide to undertake. Plan your work days to avoid working in extreme heat. If you must work on hot days, take frequent breaks and drink plenty of fluids.

Tips for Working Safely ▸

- Work with a helper whenever you can. If you have to work alone, inform a friend or family member so he or she can check up on you periodically. If you own a portable phone, keep it handy at all times.
- Use cordless power tools when they will do the job. Power cords are a frequent cause of worksite accidents. When using corded tools, plug them into a GFCI extension cord.
- Never work with tools if you have consumed alcohol or medication.
- Do not use power tools for tasks that require you to work overhead. Either find another way to access the task or substitute hand tools.

Wear sensible clothing and protective equipment when working outdoors, including a cap to protect against direct sunlight, eye protection when working with tools or chemicals, a particle mask when sanding, work gloves, full-length pants, and a long-sleeved shirt. A tool organizer turns a five-gallon bucket into a safe and convenient container for transporting tools.

Worksite Safety

Set up your worksite for quick disposal of waste materials. Use a wheelbarrow to transfer waste to a dumpster or trash can immediately. *Note: Disposal of building materials is regulated in most areas. Check with your local waste management department.*

Create a storage surface for tools. Set a sheet of plywood on top of a pair of sawhorses to make a surface for keeping tools off the ground, where they are a safety hazard and are exposed to damage from moisture. A storage surface also makes it easy for you to locate a tool when needed.

Using Ladders

Do not stand on upper steps of stepladders, particularly when handling heavy loads.

Provide level, stable footing for extension ladders. Install sturdy blocking under ladder legs if the ground is uneven, soft, or slippery, and always drive a stake next to each ladder foot to keep the ladder from slipping away from the house.

Basic Hand Tools

You probably already own many of the basic hand and power tools needed to complete the projects shown in this book. Others, such as a flooring nailer, you may have to rent. For almost every project in this book, start with a tool kit consisting of the basic tools listed below, and add specialty tools as needed.

Whenever you build outdoor projects, like porches and patios, use exterior-rated building materials and hardware whenever available. If you must use nonexterior-rated wood, like finish-grade pine, be sure to prime and paint it thoroughly.

Tools & Materials ▸

Tape measure
Pencil
Chalk line
Level

Wood chisel
Hammer
Circular saw
Drill and bits

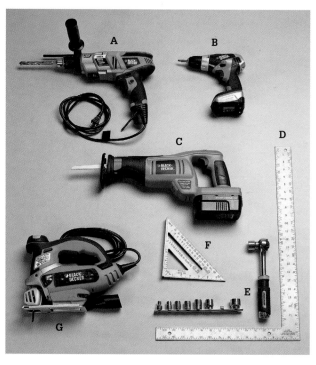

Tools for building porches and patio rooms include:
Hammer drill (A); Cordless drill/driver (B); Reciprocating saw (C); Carpenter's square (D); Ratchet wrench and sockets (E); Speed square (F); Jigsaw (G).

How to Use a Speed Square

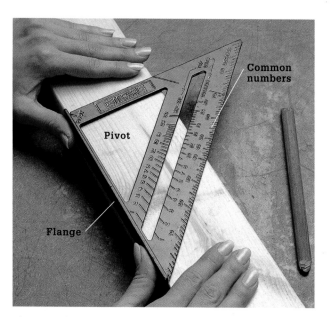

The speed square is a traditional roofer's tool that is very helpful for any projects that involve angle cutting. To use a speed square, you must either know or measure the slope of the line you want to mark, in inches per foot. Once you have the slope information, begin marking a cutting line onto a board by holding the flange of the speed square against the edge of the board. Look for the word common and the row of numbers aligned with it. Holding the end of the flange securely against the edge of the board, pivot the square so the common number equaling the rise of slope in inches per foot aligns with the same edge being pivoted against. Mark cutting line along the marking edge.

Materials for building porch and patio rooms include: Composite 2 × 4 (nonstructural) (A); Hardwood strips for screen frames (B); Fir porch floorboards (C); Construction lumber (D); Finish-grade lumber (E); T1-11 siding (F); Pre-primed plywood siding (G); Plywood (H); 6 × 6 treated post (I); 4 × 4 treated posts (J); 2× treated construction lumber (K); 2× cedar construction lumber (L).

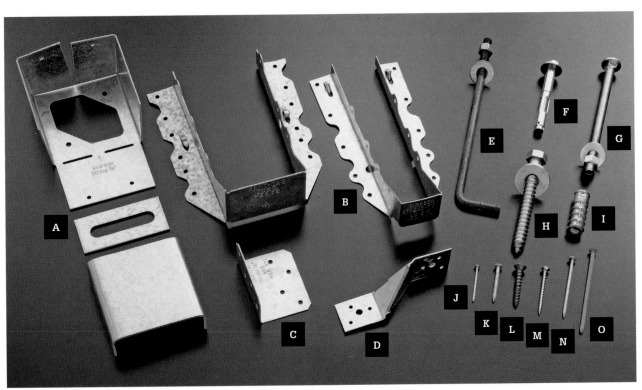

Connectors and fasteners include: standoff post anchor (A), double- and single-joist hangers (B), angle bracket (C), rafter tie (D), J-bolt with nut and washer (E), masonry anchor bolt (F), carriage bolt with nut and washer (G), lag screw with washer (H), lead anchor sleeve (I), 4d galvanized nail (J), galvanized joist-hanger nail (K), self-tapping masonry screw (L), deck screw (M), 8d galvanized nail (N), and 16d galvanized nail (O).

Front Porches

Adding a front porch to your house is a major project. But with thorough preparation and a detailed construction plan, a successful porch-building project can be accomplished by most do-it-yourselfers.

A porch is a permanent part of your home, so make sure the foundation and structure are sturdy and meet all local building codes. Also pay close attention to design issues so the size and style of the porch make sense with the rest of your house. Use the techniques illustrated in this project as a guide to help you convert your own porch plan into a reality.

This section shows:

- How to Install Ledger Boards & Posts
- How to Install Deck Joists
- How to Install Porch Floors
- How to Install Beams & Trusses
- How to Install Roof Coverings
- How to Wrap Posts & Beams
- How to Install a Cornice
- How to Finish the Cornice & Gable
- How to Install Gable Trim
- How to Install Soffits
- How to Install a Porch Ceiling

After

Before

A front porch provides a sheltered entry point and creates a pleasant outdoor living space. Adding a new front porch gives your house a more sophisticated appearance.

Anatomy of a Porch

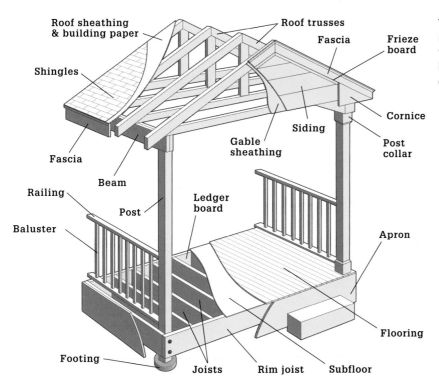

Labels (clockwise): Roof sheathing & building paper, Roof trusses, Fascia, Frieze board, Shingles, Cornice, Siding, Post collar, Gable sheathing, Fascia, Beam, Apron, Railing, Ledger board, Post, Baluster, Flooring, Footing, Joists, Rim joist, Subfloor

The basic parts of a porch include the roof, the posts and beams, the floor and floor deck, the support system (ledger board and post footings), trim, and optional elements like railings and steps.

Building Front Porches

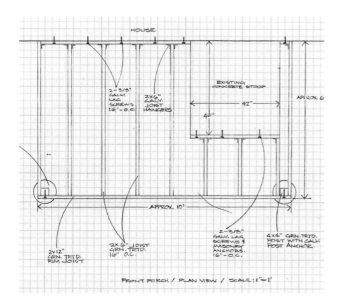

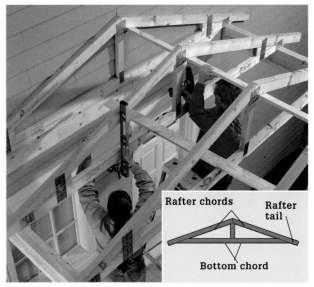

Rafter chords · Rafter tail · Bottom chord

Work from a construction plan. Because a porch is a permanent part of your house, you will need a building permit and a detailed construction plan before you start. The plan should include a plan view, like the one shown above, and an elevation drawing(s). For your convenience, also create a comprehensive materials list and an assembly plan.

Use prebuilt roof trusses for porch construction. They are easier to work with than site-built rafters. When ordering trusses, you must know the roof pitch, the distance to be spanned, and the amount of overhang past the beams. Trusses can be purchased in stock sizes or custom-ordered at most building centers. Consult with the salesperson to make sure you get the right trusses for your project.

Elements of a Porch: The Foundation

Concrete footings, cast in tubular forms, support the porch posts. Post anchors, held in place with J-bolts, secure the posts to the footings. Frost footings, required for porches, should be deep enough to extend below the frost line, where they are immune to shifting caused by freezing and thawing.

Existing concrete steps with sturdy footings can be used to support the porch deck—an easier option than removing the concrete steps. Excavate around the steps to make sure there is a footing and that it is in good condition.

Elements of a Porch: The Deck & Floor

A series of parallel joists supports the floor. Joist hangers anchor the joists to the ledger and the front rim joist, which acts like a beam to help support both the joists and the floor. Local building codes may contain specific requirements for thickness of the lumber used to make the rim joist. The face of the rim joist often is covered with finish-grade lumber, called an "apron," for a cleaner appearance.

Tongue-and-groove porch boards installed over a plywood subfloor is common porch-floor construction. The subfloor is attached to the joists. The porch boards, usually made of fir, are nailed to the subfloor with a floor nailer tool.

Elements of a Porch: The Posts & Beams

The posts and beams support the weight of the porch. Posts are secured by post anchors at the footings. Beams are connected to the posts with post saddles, and attached to a ledger board at the house using double-joist hangers. For most porch projects, doubled 2 × 6s or 2 × 8s can be used to build beams.

Wraps for posts and beams give the rough framing lumber a smoother, more finished appearance, and they also make them look more substantial and in proportion with the rest of the porch. Use finish-grade 1 × 6 and 1 × 4 pine to wrap 4 × 4 posts.

Elements of a Porch: The Roof

The porch roof is supported and given its shape by sloped rafters or trusses. Prebuilt trusses, like those shown above, are increasingly popular among do-it-yourselfers. The ends of the trusses or rafters extend past the porch beams to create an overhang that often is treated with a soffit. The trusses or rafters provide support and a nailing surface for the roof sheathing, a layer of building paper, and the roofing materials—like asphalt shingles. The area of the porch below the peak of the roof, called the "gable," is usually covered with plywood sheathing and siding. Metal flashing is installed between the roof and the house to keep water away from the walls.

Techniques for Building Porches

Ledger boards and posts support the roof and the deck of a porch. A ledger board is a sturdy piece of lumber, usually a 2 × 6 or 2 × 8, that is secured to the wall of a house to support joists or rafters for the porch. The posts used in most porch projects are 4 × 4 or 6 × 6 lumber that is attached to concrete footings with post-anchor hardware. Proper installation of the posts and ledgers is vital to the strength of the porch.

In most cases, porches are built with posts at the front only. A ledger is installed at deck level to support the floor, and another is sometimes installed at ceiling level to anchor the beams and the rafters or trusses.

If you are building your porch over an old set of concrete steps, make a cutout in the deck-level ledger board that is the same width and position as the steps, and attach the cut section to the top of the top step with masonry anchors.

Tools & Materials ▶

Basic hand tools	Shingles
Caulk gun	Roofing supplies
Framing square	Drip edge flashing
Mason's string	Caulk
Straightedge	Concrete
Plumb bob	Tubular form
Construction plans	Post anchor
Lumber	Joist-hanger nails
Plywood	Lag screws
Flooring	Speed square
Flooring nailer	Jigsaw
Nailset	Mallet
Prebuilt trusses	Duplex nails
Building paper	Line level
Flashing	J-bolt

How to Install Ledger Boards & Posts

Lay out the location for the porch ledger board, based on your project plans. Mark the center of the project area onto the wall of your house to use as a reference point for establishing the layout. Measure out from the center and mark the endpoints of the ledger location. Make another mark ½" outside the endpoint to mark cutting lines for siding removal. According to most codes, the siding must be removed before the ledger board is installed.

Mark the ledger height at the centerline. If you are building over old steps, the top of the ledger should be even with the back edge of the steps. Use a straightedge and a level to extend the height mark out to the endpoints of the ledger location. Mark cutting lines for the ledger board cutout on the siding, ½" above the ledger location, then measure down from the top cutting line a distance equal to the width of the ledger board plus 1". Mark the bottom of the cutout area at that point, and extend the mark across the project area with the level and straightedge.

Remove the siding at the cutting lines. For wood siding, set the blade of a circular saw so it cuts to the thickness of the siding, and cut along the cutting lines. Finish the cuts at the corners with a wood chisel. Remove the siding. You do not generally need to remove the wall sheathing between the siding and the framing members.

Cut a piece of metal or vinyl drip edge flashing to fit the length of the cutout area. Apply caulk or exterior panel adhesive to the back face of the flashing—do not use fasteners to attach it. Slip the flashing behind the siding at the top of the cutout.

Cut a ledger board to the size specified in your construction plan. Because the end of the outer deck joist at each side of the project will butt against the wall sheathing in most cases, ledgers should be cut 4" shorter than the full planned width of the porch to create a 2" gap for the joist at each end. Also, cut the rim joist for the porch (usually from 2 × 12 lumber) according to your project plans. Lay the ledger board next to the rim joist to gang-mark deck joist locations onto the ledger and the rim joist. To allow for the difference in length between the ledger and the rim joist, set a 2 × 6 spacer at each end of the ledger. Mark the deck joist locations onto the ledger and the rim joist according to your construction plan. In the project above, we gang-marked deck joist locations 16" apart on center, starting 15¼" in from one end of the rim joist.

(continued)

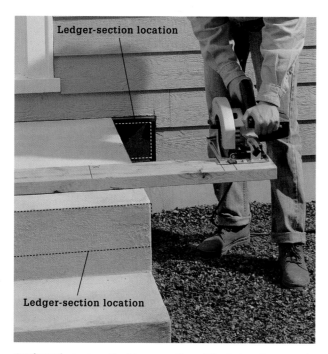

Option: If you are attaching a section of the ledger to concrete steps (page 81), set the ledger in position on the back of the steps, and mark cutting lines onto the full-length ledger board at the edges of the steps. Cut at the cutting lines to divide the ledger into three sections.

Position the ledger board in the cutout area, up against the drip edge flashing. Tack in place with duplex nails. Drill two counterbored pilot holes into the ledger at framing member locations or at 16" intervals if attaching at the rim joist. Drive $3/8 \times 4$" lag screws, with washers, into the pilot holes to secure the ledger. Install all ledger sections that attach to the wall.

Establish square lines for the sides of the porch. First, build 3-piece 2 × 4 frames, called "batter boards," and drive one into the ground at each side, 12" past the front of the project area, aligned with the project edge. Drive a nail near each end of the ledger, and tie a mason's string to each nail. Tie the other end of each string to a batter board. Square the string with the ledger using the 3-4-5 method: mark the ledger board 3 ft. from the nail, then mark the mason's string 4 ft. out from the same point. Adjust the mason's string until the endpoints from the 3-ft. and 4-ft. marks are exactly 5 ft. apart, then retie.

8

Mark locations for the centers of the porch posts onto the mason's strings by measuring out from the ledger board using your construction plan as a guide. Use a piece of tape to mark the mason's string. Make sure the mason's string is taut.

9

Transfer the location for the post centers to the ground by hanging a plumb bob from the post marks on the mason's string. Drive a stake at the post-center location, then set an 8"-diameter (or larger if codes require) tubular concrete form onto the ground, centered around the stake. Mark the edges of the form onto the ground, then remove the form and the stake, and dig a hole for the form past the frost-line depth. Avoid moving the mason's string. Set the tubular form into the hole so the top is about 2" above ground. Use a level to make sure the form is horizontal. Excavate for and install both tubular forms.

(continued)

10

Fill the tubular forms with fresh concrete. Smooth the surface of the concrete with a trowel or float, then insert a J-bolt into the fresh concrete. Use a plumb bob to find the point on the surface of the concrete that is directly below the tape mark on each mason's string. Insert a J-bolt into the concrete at that point. The threaded end of the J-bolt should extend up at least 2". Let the concrete cure for three days.

11

Set a metal post anchor over the J-bolt, and secure with a washer and nut. *Note: Standoff post anchors have a pedestal that fits over the J-bolt to support the post. Cut a post that is at least 6" longer than the planned post height. With a helper, set the post into the post anchor and secure with 10d galvanized nails driven through the pilot holes in the post anchor. Install both posts.*

12

Brace each post with a pair of 2 × 4s attached to the stakes driven in line with the edges of the posts, but outside of the project area. Secure the posts to the stakes with deck screws, then use a level to make sure the posts are plumb. Attach the braces to the posts with deck screws.

How to Install Deck Joists

1

Level line

With post braces still in place, run a mason's string between a post and the end of the ledger. Use a line level to make sure the string is level, then measure down ⅛" for every foot of distance between the ledger and the post to establish a slope line. Mark a slope line on each post.

2

Cut outer joists to fit between the back of the ledger and the front of each post using the angle created by the slope line and the post as a guide for cutting the ends of the joists. Attach the outer joists to the ends of the ledger and the posts with deck screws. You may need to bend up the drip edge flashing above the ledger.

3

Ledger

Step ledger (uninstalled)

Attach joist hangers to the ledger and to the rim joist at the joist locations with galvanized joist-hanger nails. *Tip: Slip a 2 × 6 scrap into each hanger before nailing to make sure the hanger holds its shape during installation.*

4

Tack the porch rim joist in position: The top of the rim joist should be flush with the tops of the outer deck joists. Drill four counterbored pilot holes through the rim joist and into each post, then drive ⅜ × 4" lag screws with washers at each pilot hole to secure the rim joist.

(continued)

5

Install metal corner brackets at each of the four inside corners to stabilize the frame. Use joist-hanger nails to fasten the corner brackets. *Note: Some local codes now require that you use a three-sided joist hanger on end joists, not a corner bracket. Check with your local building department.*

6

Cut the remaining deck joists that fit all the way from the ledger to the porch rim joist. Cut the same end angles that were cut for the outer joists. Install the deck joists in the joist hangers with joist-hanger nails.

Lag screw

Masonry anchor sleeve

Option: If you are building over old steps, attach the step ledger board to the riser of the top step, using masonry anchors (inset). Lay a straightedge across the joists next to the steps as a reference for aligning the top of the ledger board. Shim under the ledger to hold it in position, then drill counterbored, ⅜"-diameter pilot holes for the lag screws into the ledger. Mark the pilot hole locations onto the riser, then remove the ledger. Drill holes for ⅜"-diameter masonry-anchor sleeves into the riser with a hammer drill and a masonry bit. Drive the sleeves into the holes with a maul or hammer, then attach the step ledger with ⅜ × 4" lag screws driven into the masonry sleeves. Drive pairs of lag screws at 16" intervals.

How to Install Porch Floors

Begin laying the plywood subfloor—we used ¾"-thick exterior plywood. Measure and cut plywood so any seams fall over deck joists, keeping a slight (⅛") expansion gap between pieces. Fasten plywood pieces with 1½" deck screws. If you are installing the floor over old steps, apply exterior-grade construction adhesive to the steps to bond with the plywood.

Notch plywood to fit around posts. Also nail a 2 × 4 nailing cleat to the edges of the post that are not fitted against joists. Make sure the cleat is level with the tops of the joists.

Notch for post

Nailing cleat

Cut a starter board from a tongue-and-groove porch board by ripcutting the grooved edge off of the board with a circular saw. Cut the starter board 1" longer than the finished length, including a ¾" overhang for the porch apron.

Set the starter board next to the post, with the tongue edge pressed against the post. Mark the location of the post onto the porch board, measure and mark the cutting depth to fit around the post, then notch the board with a jigsaw.

(continued)

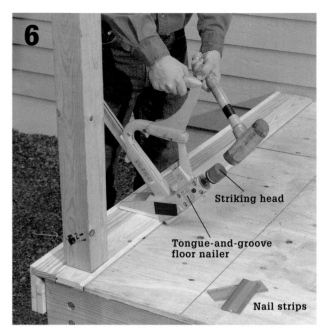

Make a cleat and spacer from scrap lumber the same thickness (usually ¾") as the skirt board you will install at the side of the porch. Sandwich the cleat and spacer together and attach them to the outer joist so the cleat is on the outside and at least 2" above the top of the joist. The spacer should be below the top of the joist. The cleat provides a secure, straight edge for aligning the first porch board, and the spacer creates an overhang for the skirt board.

Butt the notched porch board (step 4, previous page) against the cleat so it fits around the post, and nail it in place. If using a tongue-and-groove floor nailer, load a nail strip, then position the nailer over the exposed tongue and rap the striking head with a mallet to discharge and set the nails. Nail at 6" to 8" intervals, then cut and position the next porch board (notched for the post, if needed) so the groove fits around the tongue of the first board, and nail in place.

Continue installing the porch boards. Draw reference lines on the subfloor, perpendicular to the house, to check the alignment of the porch boards. Measure from a porch board to the nearest reference line occasionally, making sure the distance is equal at all points. Adjust the position of the next board(s), if needed.

Notch the porch boards to fit around the other front post before you install them, then ripcut the last board to fit (create an overhang equal to the starter-board overhang). Position the last board, and drive galvanized finish nails through the face of the board and into the subfloor. Set the nail heads with a nail set.

9

¾" overhang

10

Front apron

Trim the exposed porch board ends so they are even. First, mark several porch boards ¾" out from the front edge of the rim joist to create an overhang that will cover the top of the apron (see next step). Snap a chalk line to connect the marks, creating a cutting line. Use a straightedge as a guide and trim off the boards at the cutting line with a circular saw. Use a hand saw to finish the cuts around the posts.

Cut aprons from exterior plywood to conceal the outer joists and the rim joist. Cut the side aprons (we used ¾"-thick plywood) so they fit flush with the front edges of the posts, then install them beneath the porch board overhangs and nail it in place with 8d siding nails. After the side aprons are in place, cut the front apron long enough to cover the edge grain on the side aprons, and nail it to the rim joist.

Option: Build a wooden step and cover the surface with porch boards. The step above was built with a framework of 2 × 8s (toenailed to the front skirt), wrapped with exterior plywood, then covered with porch boards.

How to Install Beams & Trusses

Measure to find the midpoint of the porch deck and mark it on the house, then transfer the centerline to the peak area of the planned roof using a straight 2 × 4 and a carpenter's level. Refer to your construction plan, then measure up from the porch deck and mark the top and bottom of the roof ledger onto the siding, near the center mark. Also mark the ledger height at the ends of the project area, then connect the height marks with a chalk line.

Mark a 2 × 6 for the roof ledger by setting it on the deck so it extends past the edges of both front posts. Mark the outside edges of the posts onto the 2 × 6, then make another mark directly above each edge of the deck. Cut the ledger to length, and make a reference mark at the midpoint of the board.

At the roof ledger outline on the wall, measure out in each direction from the centerpoint and finish the outline so it is the same length as the ledger board. Enlarge the outline by ½" on all sides, then remove the siding in the outlined area. Use an electronic stud finder to locate the framing members.

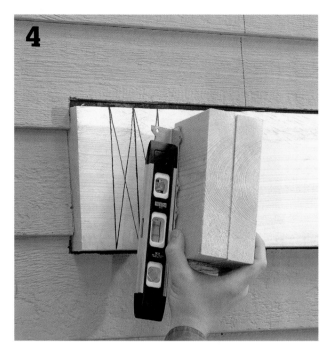

4

5

Attach the roof ledger with pairs of ⅜ × 4" lag screws driven at the framing member locations. Lay out the locations for the beams onto the ledger, according to your construction plan. Insert a pair of 2 × 8 scraps into the double-joist hanger to help it keep its shape when you nail it. Position the hanger against the ledger, using a torpedo level to make sure it is plumb. Fasten the double-joist hangers to the ledger with joist-hanger nails.

Mark the front posts at the height of the bottoms of the double-joist hangers. To make sure the marks are level, set a straight board in each joist hanger and hold the free end against the post. Use a carpenter's level to adjust the height of the board until it is level, then mark the post where it meets the bottom of the straight board. Draw cutting lines on all sides of the post at the height mark.

6

7

Steady the post, and trim off the top at the cutting line. *Safety Tip: Have a helper brace the post from below, but be careful not to drop the cutoff post end in the area.*

Make the beams (we used pairs of 2 × 8s cut to length, then nailed together with 16d common nails). The beams should extend from the double-joist hangers, past the fronts of the posts (1½" in our project). When nailing boards together to make beams, space nails in rows of three, every 12" to 16". For extra holding power, drive the nails at a slight angle.

(continued)

8

Lay out truss locations onto the tops of the beams, starting at the beam ends that will fit into the joist hangers. Mark both edges of each truss, drawing an "X" between the lines for reference. Generally, trusses should be spaced at 24" intervals—check your construction plan for exact placement.

9

Set a metal post saddle onto the top of each front post, and nail in place with joist-hanger nails. With a helper, raise the beams and set them into the post saddles and double-joist hangers. Secure the beams in the double-joist hangers with joist-hanger nails.

10

Spacer

If your beams are thinner than your posts (as above), cut plywood spacers and install them between the inside edges of the beams and the inner flange of the post saddle. The spacers should fit snugly and be trimmed to roughly the size of the saddle flanges. Drive joist-hanger nails through the caps and into the spacers and beams.

11

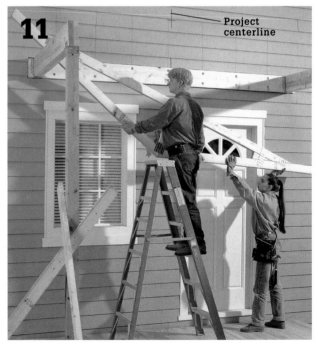

Project centerline

With help, hoist the first truss into position. Turn the trusses upside down to make them easier to handle when raising. Rest one end of the truss on a beam, then slide the other end up and onto the opposite beam. Invert the truss so the peak points upward, and position it against the house, with the peak aligned on the project centerline.

12

Rafter chords

Bottom chord

Make sure the first truss is flush against the siding, with the peak aligned on the project centerline. Nail the rafter chords and bottom chord of the truss to the house at framing member locations using 20d common nails. Lift the remaining trusses onto the beams.

13

Install the rest of the trusses at the locations marked on the beams, working away from the house, by toenailing through the bottom chords and into the beams with 8d nails. Nail the last truss flush with the ends of the beams. *Note: If the bottom chord of the first truss overhangs the beams, install the rest of the trusses with equal overhangs.*

14

1 × 4 brace

Attach 1 × 4 braces to the underside of each row of rafter chords. Use a level to plumb each truss before fastening it to the braces with 2" deck screws.

How to Install Roof Coverings

Cut and attach 2 × 4 nailing strips to the rafter chords of the front truss using 2½" deck screws. Nailing strips create a nailing surface for the roof sheathing overhang. Cut them to the same dimensions as the rafter chords.

Cut ¾" exterior-grade plywood roof sheathing. The sheathing should be flush with the ends of the rafter tails. Cut sheathing pieces so seams fall over rafter locations, and install them with 8d siding nails or deck screws.

Fill in the rest of the sheathing, saving the pieces that butt together at the peak for last. Leave a ¼" gap at the peak.

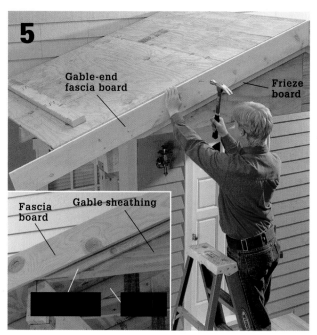

Cut ½"-thick plywood to cover the gable end of the roof. Measure the triangular shape of the gable end, from the bottom of the truss to the bottoms of the nailing strips. Divide the area into two equal-sized triangular areas, and cut the plywood to fit. Butt the pieces together directly under the peak, and attach them to the front truss with 1½" deck screws.

Cut 1 × 4 frieze boards to fit against the plywood gable sheathing beneath the nailing strips. Attach the frieze boards to the gable sheathing with 1" deck screws. Then, cut fascia boards long enough to extend several inches past the ends of the rafter tails. Nail the fascia boards to the nailing strips, with the tops flush with the tops of the roof sheathing.

Measure for side fascia boards that fit between the house and the back faces of the gable-end fascia boards. Cut the fascia boards to fit, then attach them with galvanized 8d finish nails driven into the ends of the rafter tails. Make sure the tops of the fascia boards do not protrude above the plane of the roof sheathing. *Note: If you plan to install soffits, use fascia boards with a dadoed groove for soffit panels.*

Trim off the ends of the gable-end fascia boards so they are flush with the side fascia boards using a handsaw. Drive two or three 8d finish nails through the gable-end fascia boards and into the ends of the side fascia boards.

(continued)

8

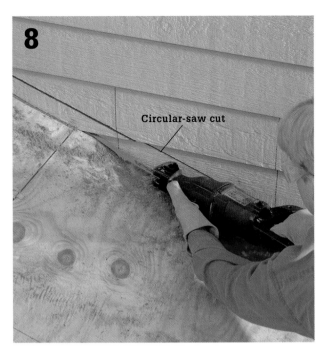

Circular-saw cut

Remove the siding above the roof sheathing to create a recess for the metal roof flashing. Make a cut about 2" above the sheathing using a circular saw with the cutting depth set to the siding thickness. Then make a cut flush with the top of the roof using a reciprocating saw held at a very low angle. Connect the cuts at the ends with a wood chisel and remove the siding. See page 56 for more information on removing siding.

9

Step flashing

Install building paper, drip edge flashing, and shingles as you would for a standard roofing project. Slip pieces of metal step flashing behind the siding above the cutout area as you finish rows of shingles, sealing the seams with roof cement.

10

Shingle tabs

Finish shingling and flashing the roof. Make sure shingle tabs are staggered in regular patterns, with a consistent exposed area on the shingle tabs. Cut off the shingle tabs and use them to create the roof ridge.

How to Wrap Posts & Beams

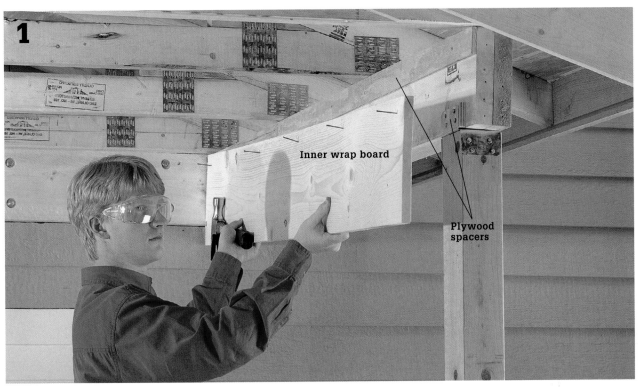

Cut the wrap boards for the inner sides of the beams to the same length as the beams using finish lumber wide enough to cover the beams and any metal saddles or joiners. We used 1 × 10, but sanded ¾" plywood can be used instead. Attach the inner wrap boards to the beams with 8d siding nails. In the project above, we added ½" plywood strips at the top and bottom of the beam to compensate for the ½" spacers in the metal post saddles.

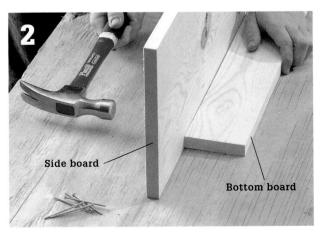

Cut strips of wood to cover the bottoms of the beams. Position each strip next to a board cut the same size as the inner beam wrap board. The difference in length between the side board and the bottom board should equal the distance of the beam overhang at the post plus the size of the post. Preassemble the bottom board and side board by driving 8d finish nails at the butt joint, making sure to keep the joint square. Attach the assembly to the beam so the free end of the bottom board forms a butt joint with the inner beam wrap board.

Cut boards to create an end cap for each beam. We cut a piece of 1 × 10 to fit over the ends of the beam and the beam wrap and attached it to a piece of 1 × 4 cut to cover the gap beneath the beam overhang. Nail end caps over the end of each beam. *Tip: For an extra tight joint that is less likely to separate, cut rabbets into the edges of the end wrap and use construction adhesive to reinforce the joint.*

(continued)

Cut boards for wrapping the posts so they span from the floor to the bottoms of the wrapped beams. For a 4 × 4 post, two 1 × 4s and two 1 × 6s per post can be used. Nail a 1 × 6 to the front of the post, overhanging ¾" on the outside edges. Nail a 1 × 4 to the outer face of the post, butted against the 1 × 6.

Preassemble the other two wrap boards, nailing through the face of the 1 × 6 and into the edge of the 1 × 4. Set the assembly around the post, nailing the 1 × 6 to the post and nailing through the other 1 × 6 and into the edge of the 1 × 4 (there will be some space between the second 1 × 4 and the post).

Cut pieces of finish lumber to fit around the bases of the posts (called "post collars"). We used 1 × 6 to create the bottom post collars, and 1 × 4 to create the top collars where the posts meet the beams. Nail the collars together with 4d finish nails. *Tip: Cut pieces so the front collar board covers the end grain of the side boards.*

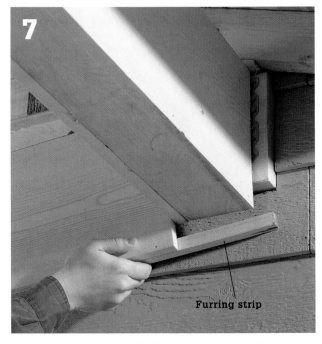

Furring strip

Roof ledgers often are visible after the porch ceiling is installed, so cover the ledger with finish lumber. If the ledger protrudes past the siding, cut a furring strip to cover the gap between the inside face of the ledger cover and the siding. Cut the ledger cover and furring strips to fit and install them with 8d nails. If the ledger extends past the outer face of the beam, the easiest solution is to paint it to match the siding.

How to Install a Cornice

At each end of the front porch, measure the area from the end of the gable fascia to a spot about 6" inside the porch beam. Lay out a triangular piece of plywood or finish-grade lumber to fit the area, using a carpenter's square to create right angles. Cut out the cornice pieces using a circular saw and straightedge.

Test-fit the cornice pieces over the ends of the porch gable, then install with 8d finish nails driven into the ends of the beams and 4d nails driven up through the ends of the cornice pieces and into the underside of the gable fascia. Use a nail set to embed the heads of the nails below the surface of the wood, being careful not to split the cornice pieces.

How to Finish the Cornice & Gable

Gable trim

Cornice

The cornice and gable are finished to match the siding and trim on your house. Use plywood or finish-grade lumber to make the cornice, and use siding that matches your house for the gable trim.

Caulk seams at the peak of the gable and between the fascia boards and the cornice.

How to Install Gable Trim

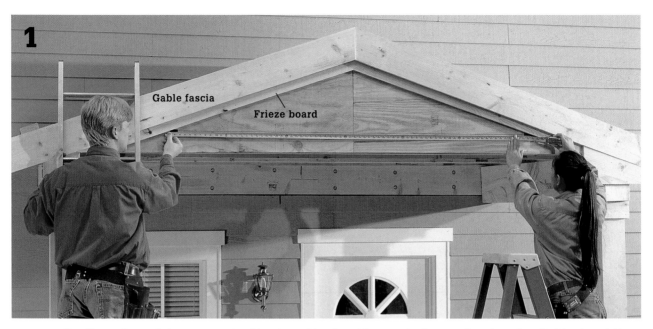

1

Gable fascia

Frieze board

Measure the dimensions of the area covered by the gable sheathing on the house. If you have installed fascia and frieze boards, measure from the bottom of the frieze boards. Overhang the bottom edge of the gable by 2" to make sure that the siding will cover the edge of the ceiling once the ceiling and soffits are installed. Snap a horizontal chalk line near the bottom of the gable sheathing to use as a reference line for installing the siding.

2

3

Mark a cutting line that matches the slope of the roof onto the end of one piece of siding. Use a framing square or a speed square (page 40) to mark the slope line. *Option: Position a scrap board on the horizontal chalk line on the gable sheathing and mark the points where the edges of the board intersect with the frieze board. Connect the points to establish the slope line. Cut the siding or scrap board on the slope line and use it as a template to mark the siding for cutting. Cut the bottom siding board to length.*

Use 4d siding nails to install the bottom siding board so it is flush with the bottom edges of the frieze boards. The bottom edge of the siding board should be 2" lower than the bottom of the gable sheathing. Cut the next siding board so it overlaps the first board from above, creating the same amount of exposed siding as in the rest of the house. Be careful to keep the siding level. Continue cutting and installing siding pieces until you reach the peak of the gable.

How to Install Soffits

1

Plowed groove

Attach a fascia board with a plowed (dadoed) groove to the rafter ends.

2

Use a torpedo level to transfer the top height of the groove to the beam near one end. Mark the groove height at the other end of the beam, then connect with a chalk line. Install a 2 × 2 nailer just above the chalk line.

3

Measure from the back of the plowed groove to the beam, just below the nailer, to find the required width of the soffit panel. Measure the length, then cut a piece of ⅜"-thick plywood to fit. Insert one edge of the soffit panel into the plow, then nail the other edge to the nailer with 4d nails.

4

Attach the soffit directly to the rafters with 4d galvanized common nails, then caulk the edges before painting the panel.

How to Install a Porch Ceiling

To create nailing surfaces for ceiling materials, cut 2 × 4s to fit between rafters, spaced 24" on center and flush with the bottoms of the rafters. *Note: If you plan to install ceiling lights, have them wired before proceeding.*

Measure the ceiling space and cut the ceiling materials to fit (we used 4 × 8 sheets of ⅜"-thick plywood). Cut the ceiling pieces so the seams fall on the centers of the rafters and nailing strips. Use 4d galvanized nails to attach the plywood to the rafters and nailers. Space nails at 8" to 12" intervals. Do not drive nails next to one another on opposite sides of joints.

Install molding around the edges of the ceiling to cover the gaps and create a more decorative look. Simple ¾" cove molding, which does not require any complicated coping cuts or installation techniques, is used for the above project. Miter the corners and attach with 4d finish nails. Set the nail heads slightly, then cover it with wood putty before painting.

Applying Finishing Touches

Use gable ornamentation to soften the hard lines of the gable peak. Fan-style trim and many other trim types that fit into a peak are made for a range of different peak angles. Make sure to measure your peak angle carefully before purchasing or ordering gable ornamentation.

Install decorative trim to enhance the appeal of your porch. The scalloped fascia boards above were cut from plain 1 × 6 pine using a jigsaw to add a touch of flair to a plain porch gable. Caulk all seams once trim is installed.

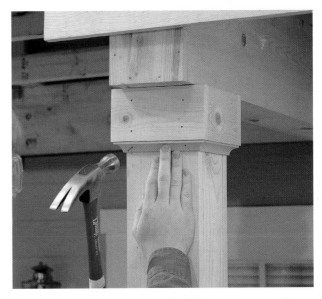

Put stock moldings sold at any building center to creative use on a porch. The simple cove molding above is installed at the joint between a post collar and the post, to create more graceful lines.

Porch Railings

A porch railing not only provides security from falls, but it can also make an important contribution to the visual appeal of a porch. The basic components of a railing are the railing posts, the bottom and top rails, the balusters, and optional cap rails. It is usually easiest to assemble the railing before you install it. Check local codes before designing a railing. In most cases, railings should be at least 36 inches high, and the spaces between balusters and between the porch floor and bottom rail should be no more than 4 inches.

Tools & Materials ▶

Basic hand tools	Post caps
Speed square	Milled rail caps
Ratchet and	Balusters
socket set	Lag screws
Plywood	Screws
Framing lumber	Siding rails

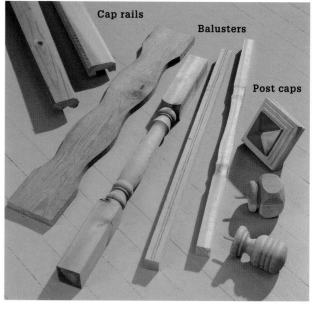

Railing components include decorative cap rails that are grooved to fit over a 2 × 2 railing; balusters, sometimes called spindles, that range from plain 2 × 2s to ornate millwork; and decorative post caps.

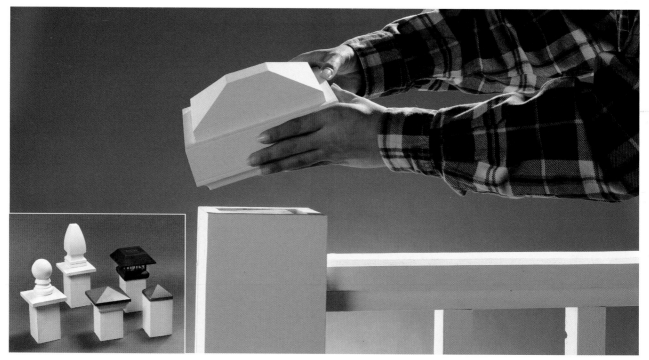

Add preformed post caps to non-bearing posts that support porch railings. Post caps are sold in a wide range of styles and sizes at most building centers. Most are attached by driving finish nails through the top of the cap and into the post. Others are screwed into the post top with preinstalled screws. You'll find many styles available (inset).

How to Build & Install a Porch Railing

1

2

Make a base plate for the railing post from two pieces of ¾"-thick plywood. Cut the plywood pieces to match the finished size of the post, including any post wrap boards. Stack the pieces together and fasten with 1¼" screws and construction adhesive. Do not put screws in corners.

Cut the post to finished height (usually 38 to 40"), allowing for the thickness of the base plate. If you plan to wrap the post, use scrap lumber the same thickness as the wrap boards to center the post on the base plate. Attach the base plate to the bottom of the post with three counterbored ⅜ × 4" lag screws.

3

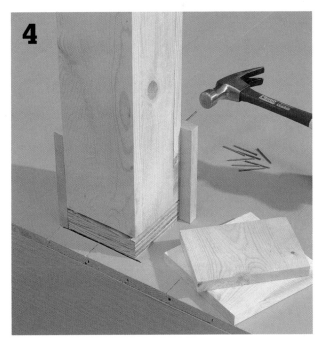

4

Set the post in position on the porch floor. Drive ⅜ × 4" lag screws through the pilot holes at each corner of the base plate and into the porch floor.

Cut and install wrap boards to match the other porch posts. Also cut and install collar boards to cover the edges of the base plate and the bottom of the post.

(continued)

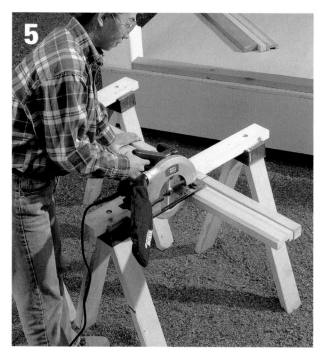

Cut the top, bottom, and cap rails to length. The bottom rail will have to be cut shorter than the top and cap rails if you have installed collars at the post base. For our railings, we used 2 × 4s for the bottom rails, 2 × 2s for the top rails, and pre-milled cap rails installed over the top rails.

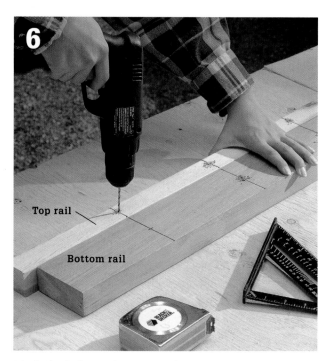

Mark the baluster layout onto the top and bottom rails—make sure balusters will be no more than 4" apart when installed. Drill a ⅛"-diameter pilot hole all the way through the rails at each baluster layout mark, centering the holes from side to side.

If you are cutting your own balusters, clamp, measure, and cut the balusters to finished length. To save time and ensure uniform length, gang-cut the balusters using a circular saw and a straightedge. Paint all railing parts with primer.

Lay the top and bottom rails on a work surface. Use shims to support the balusters and the top rail so they align with the center of the bottom rail. Attach the balusters to the rails by driving 2½" deck screws through the pilot holes in the rails and into the baluster ends. *Tip: Use a spacing block to keep balusters from spinning when they are attached.*

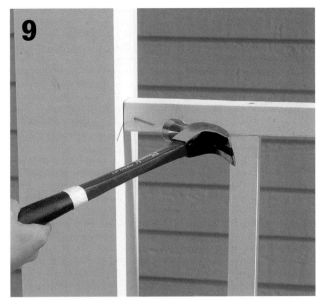

Insert the railing assembly between posts, using blocks to support it at the desired height. Drill ⅛" angled holes through the ends of the top and bottom rails and into the posts. Toenail railings to posts with 8d casing nails.

Slip the cap rail over the top rail. Attach the cap rail by driving 2½" deck screws at 18" intervals up through the top rail and into the cap rail.

How to Install a Porch Rail Between Round Posts

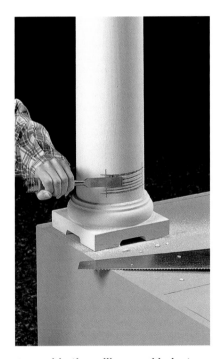

Assemble the railings and balusters. Position the assembly between the posts. Mark the top and bottom of each rail onto the posts. Cut along the lines with a handsaw, then use a chisel to remove wood between the cuts so the receiving surface is flat for the rail ends.

Install the railing assembly by inserting the rail ends into the post notches. Pre-drill and toenail the rail ends to the posts.

Set a compass to the post radius, then scribe an arc cutting line on each end of a cap rail. The distance between the arcs should equal the distance between posts. Cut along the cutting lines with a jigsaw. Attach the cap rail to the top rail (step 10, above).

Wood Porch Steps

Wood porch steps consist of three basic parts: stringers, usually made from 2 × 12s, provide the framework and support for the steps; treads, made from 2 × 12s or pairs of 2 × 6s, are the stepping surfaces; and risers, usually made from 2 × 8s, are the vertical boards at the back of each step.

If you are replacing steps, use the dimensions of the old steps as a guide. If not, you will need to create a plan for the new steps, which takes a little bit of math and a little bit of trial and error (see next page).

In addition to the step dimensions, consider style issues when designing steps, and if there are two or more steps, include a step railing that matches your existing porch railing.

Porch steps should be at least 3 ft. wide. Try to match the width of the sidewalk at the base of the step area. To inhibit warping and provide better support, use three stringers, not two. Wood steps do not require footings in most jurisdictions (check with your building department). Simply attach them to the rim joist or apron of the porch, and anchor them to the sidewalk at the base of the first step.

Tools & Materials ▶

Basic hand tools	Milled cap rail
Framing square	Corner brackets
Hand saw	Carriage bolts
Pressure-treated lumber	Self-tapping concrete screws
Finish lumber	Deck screws

Wooden porch steps are easier to build and less expensive than concrete steps. With paint and the appropriate railing design, they can also be made to match the look of the porch.

Building Steps

Remove the old steps, if any, from the project area. With the old steps removed, you can better evaluate the structure of the porch to make a plan for anchoring the new steps. If possible, attach the step stringers directly to the porch rim joist or to the apron. Also evaluate the condition of the sidewalk to make sure it is strong enough to support the steps.

Make a detailed plan for the steps, keeping in mind that each step should be 10 to 12" deep, with riser height between 6 and 8". Make sure the planned steps conform to the required overall rise and run (photos, below). *Note: When designing railings, make sure the space between individual balusters is less than 4".*

How to Measure Rise & Run

1

Overall run

Attach a mason's string to the porch floor. Drive a stake where you want the base of the bottom step to fall. Attach the other end of the string to the stake, and use a line level to level it. Measure the length of the string—this distance is the overall run of the steps.

2

Overall rise

Measure down from the string to the bottom of the stake to determine the overall height, or rise, of the steps. Divide the overall rise by the estimated number of steps. The rise of each step should be between 6 and 8". For example, if the overall rise is 21" and you plan to build three steps, the rise of each step would be 7". It is very important that all risers and all treads are uniform in size.

How to Build Porch Steps

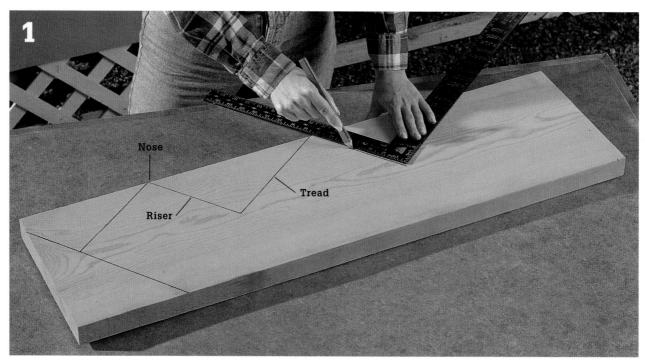

Mark the step layout onto a pressure-treated board—usually a 2 × 12—to make the step stringers. Use a carpenter's square with the rise distance and run distance each noted on a leg of the square. Lay out the stringer so the "nose" areas where the tread and riser meet on each step fall at the same edge of the board. Check all angles with the square to make sure they are right angles.

Cut out the stringer using a circular saw for straight cuts and finishing the cuts with a handsaw where cuts meet at inside corners. Use this stringer as a template for laying out and cutting two more stringers. Mark and trim off the thickness of one tread (1½") at the bottom of each stringer so the rise of the bottom step will equal the rise of the other steps.

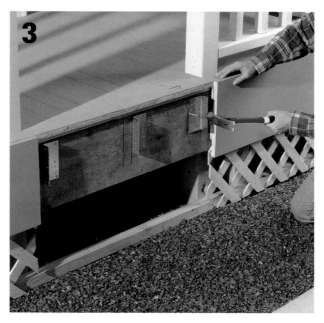

Attach evenly spaced metal angle brackets to the porch rim joist or apron, making sure the brackets are perpendicular to the ground. Position the stringers inside the angle brackets so the top of each stringer is 1½" below the top of the porch floor. Attach the stringers to the angle brackets with joist-hanger nails.

Measure the distances between the stringer tops, then use these measurements to cut two 2 × 4 cleats to length from pressure-treated lumber. Making sure stringers are square to the rim joist, attach the cleats to the concrete between the bases of the stringers, using self-tapping concrete screws driven into pilot holes. Face-nail the outside stringers to the cleat ends and toenail the middle stringer.

Cut posts for the step railing to height, and attach them to the outside face of an outer stringer using 6" carriage bolts. Use a level to set the posts so they are plumb, then clamp them in position while you drill guide holes for the carriage bolts through the posts and the stringer. Drive the carriage bolts through the guide holes and secure each with a washer and nut on the inside face of the stringer.

Cut the risers and treads to length using a circular saw. A 1" to 2" overhang at each outer stringer creates more attractive steps. Notch the treads for the top and bottom steps to fit around the posts using a jigsaw. Attach the risers to the vertical edges of the stringers using 2½" deck screws, then attach the treads.

(continued)

Mark a 2 × 4 to use for the lower railing. To mark the 2 × 4 for cutting, lay it on the steps flush against the posts, then mark a cutting line on the 2 × 4 at each inside post edge. Use the 2 × 4 as a template for marking cutting lines on the top and the cap rails.

Set the blade of a circular saw or power miter saw to match the angle of the cutting marks on the 2 × 4, and gang the 2 × 4 with a 2 × 2 for the top railing and a piece of cap rail for cutting. Gang-cut the rails at the cutting lines.

Attach the bottom rail to the posts with 2½" deck screws driven through pilot holes and into the inside faces of the posts. The bottom of the rail should be level with the noses of the steps. Attach the 2 × 2 top rail so it is parallel to the bottom rail, 2" down from the finished post height.

Hold a 2 × 2 flush against a post so the ends extend past the top and bottom rails. Mark cutting lines on the 2 × 2 at the bottom edge of the top rail and the top edge of the bottom rail. Use the 2 × 2 as a template for marking cutting lines on all railing balusters.

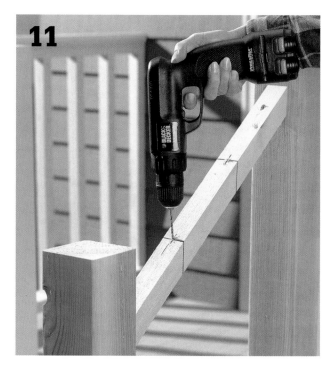

Mark layout lines for the balusters on the top and bottom rails, spacing the balusters no more than 4" apart. Drill ⅛" holes in the center of the top rail at baluster locations, then drive 2½" deck screws into the baluster ends. Toenail balusters to the bottom rail with 8d finish nails. Attach the cap rail.

Install a bottom rail, top rail, and cap rail in a horizontal position between the railing post at the top step and the end post for the porch railing. If the distance between posts is more than 4", install balusters between the rails.

Nailing strip

Close off any open areas under the stringers with wood or lattice panels. First, attach nailing strips to the undersides of the outer stringer that are set back far enough to create a recess for the wood or lattice. Cut a piece of wood or lattice to fit, and install. Attach decorative post caps if desired, but first double-check the step post tops with a straightedge to make sure the tops follow the slope of the railing. Trim one or both post tops to height, if necessary.

Platforms for Steps & Decking

This simple platform is a popular option for sheds because it's so easy to build, and it provides a sturdy step for comfortable access. You can use the same basic design to make platforms of any size. A large platform can become an outdoor sitting area, while a stack of smaller platforms can create a set of steps that are accessible from three directions. For stability and longevity, set your platforms on top of solid concrete blocks—the same type used for block foundations.

Tools & Materials ▸

Shovel	Drill	16d galvanized	2× treated lumber
Level	Compactible gravel	common nails	3" deck screws
Saw	(optional)		

How to Build a Basic Platform

STEP 1: BUILD THE PLATFORM FRAME

A. Cut two long side pieces from 2 × 6 lumber. These should equal the total length of the frame. Cut two end pieces to fit between the side pieces. For example, if your platform will measure 24 × 36", cut the sides at 36" and cut the ends at 23". Also cut an intermediate support for every 16" in between: make these the same length as the end pieces.

B. Fasten the end pieces between the sides with pairs of 16d galvanized common nails.

C. Fasten the intermediate support at the center of the frame or at 16" intervals.

Assemble the frame pieces with pairs of 16d common nails.

STEP 2: INSTALL THE DECKING

A. Cut 2 × 6 decking boards to fit the long dimension of the platform frame (or use ⁵⁄₄ × 6 decking boards).

B. Measure the frame diagonally from corner to corner to make sure it is square.

C. Starting at the front edge of the frame, attach the decking to the framing pieces with pairs of 3" deck screws. Leave a ¼" gap between the boards. Rip the last board to width so that it overhangs the front edge of the frame by 1".

D. Set the platform in position on top of the block foundation. If desired, fasten the platform to the shed with 3" screws.

Install the decking with screws, leaving a ¼" gap between boards.

Concrete Steps

Designing steps requires some calculations and some trial and error. As long as the design meets safety guidelines, you can adjust elements such as the landing depth and the dimensions of the steps. Sketching your plan on paper will make the job easier.

Before demolishing your old steps, measure them to see if they meet safety guidelines. If so, you can use them as a reference for your new steps. If not, start from scratch so your new steps do not repeat any design errors.

For steps with more than two risers, you'll need to install a handrail. Ask your local building inspector about other requirements.

Tools & Materials ▸

Tape measure	Concrete mixing tools	Steel rebar grid	Exterior-grade ¾" plywood
Sledge hammer	Jigsaw	Wire	Isolation board
Shovel	Clamps	Bolsters	#3 rebar
Drill	Ruler or framing square	Construction adhesive	Stakes
Level	Float	Compactible gravel	Vegetable oil
Mason's string	Step edger	Fill material	or commercial
Hand tamper	Broom	2" deck screws	release agent
Mallet	2 × 4 lumber		

New concrete steps give a fresh, clean appearance to your house. And if your old steps are unstable, replacing them with concrete steps that have a nonskid surface will create a safer living environment.

How to Build Concrete Steps

Remove or demolish the existing steps; if the old steps are concrete, set aside the rubble to use as fill material for the new steps. Wear protective gear, including eye protection and gloves, when demolishing concrete.

Dig 12"-wide trenches to the required depth for footings. Locate the trenches perpendicular to the foundation, spaced so the footings will extend 3" beyond the outside edges of the steps. Install steel rebar grids for reinforcement. Affix isolation boards to the house's foundation wall inside each trench using a few dabs of construction adhesive.

Mix the concrete and pour the footings. Level and smooth the concrete with a screed board. You do not need to float the surface afterwards.

When bleed water disappears, insert 12" sections of No. 3 rebar 6" into the concrete, spaced at 12" intervals and centered side to side. Leave 1 ft. of clear space at each end.

Let the footings cure for two days, then excavate the area between them to 4" deep. Pour in a 5"-thick layer of compactable gravel subbase and tamp until it is level with the footings.

6

Make slope ⅛" per foot

Transfer the measurements for the side forms from your working sketch onto ¾" exterior-grade plywood. Cut out the forms along the cutting lines using a jigsaw. Save time by clamping two pieces of plywood together and cutting both side forms at the same time. Add a ⅛" per foot back-to-front slope to the landing part of the form.

7

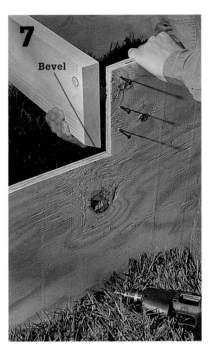

Bevel

Cut form boards for the risers to fit between the side forms. Bevel the bottom edges of the boards when cutting to create clearance for the float at the back edges of the steps. Attach the riser forms to the side forms with 2" deck screws.

8

Cleats

Riser support

Cut a 2 × 4 to make a center support for the riser forms. Use 2" deck screws to attach 2 × 4 cleats to the riser forms, then attach the support to the cleats. Check to make sure all corners are square.

9

Cut an isolation board and glue it to the house foundation at the back of the project area. Set the form onto the footings, flush against the isolation board. Add 2 × 4 bracing arms to the sides of the form, attaching them to cleats on the sides and to stakes driven into the ground.

(continued)

Fill the form with clean fill (broken concrete or rubble). Stack the fill carefully, keeping it 6" away from the sides, back, and top edges of the form. Shovel smaller fragments onto the pile to fill the void areas.

Lay pieces of No. 3 metal rebar on top of the fill at 12" intervals, and attach them to the bolsters with wire to keep them from rolling when the concrete is poured. Keep the rebar at least 4" below the top of the forms. Mist the forms and the rubble with water.

Mix concrete and pour steps one at a time, beginning at the bottom. Settle and smooth the concrete with a screed board. Press a piece of No. 3 rebar 1" down near the nose of each tread for reinforcement.

Float the steps, working the front edge of the float underneath the beveled edge at the bottom of each riser form.

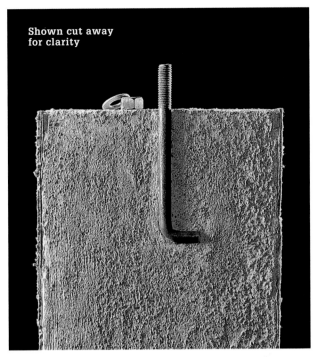

Shown cut away for clarity

Pour concrete into the forms for the remaining steps and the landing. Press rebar near the nose of each step. Keep an eye on the poured concrete as you work, and stop to float any concrete as soon as the bleed water disappears.

Option: For railings with mounting plates that attach to sunken J-bolts, install the bolts before the concrete sets. Otherwise, choose railings with surface-mounted hardware (see step 16) that can be attached after the steps are completed.

Mounting plate

Once the concrete sets, shape the step noses and landing with a step edger. Float the surface. Sweep with a stiff-bristled broom for maximum traction.

Remove the forms after the concrete has set overnight. Backfill the area around the base of the steps, and seal the concrete. Caulk between the house and the concrete steps. Install a railing.

Portico

One effective way to improve your home's street appeal, while providing a sheltered entryway, is to build a portico. Many of the same techniques used to build a porch can be used to build a portico. Because a portico typically covers separate steps and a landing, it has no deck. Some have side walls and front walls, but more often you will see them open on all three sides. They can range greatly in size and style, from a very modest add-on like the project featured here, to a two-story extravaganza with massive architectural columns.

Portico posts usually are fastened directly to the concrete steps with masonry fasteners and post anchors. The edges of the post anchors should be a minimum of 2" from the edges of the steps. If you are attaching posts to concrete steps, make sure they have footings that extend below the frost line. Check with your local building inspector for specific codes and regulations in your area.

To build the roof structure, you can choose to make rafters using traditional carpentry techniques or you can eliminate some of that trickiness by purchasing prefabricated trusses instead. When ordering trusses, make sure you know the roof pitch, truss span (the distance from the outside edge of one beam to the other), and the rafter tail overhang (typically 12"). Also let the truss manufacturer know of any special design details you'd like, such as scissor trusses to create a slightly vaulted ceiling.

Your portico project will require a building permit. Draw up detailed, specific plans (elevation and floor plan at a minimum) as well as a cost estimate to present to your local building inspector.

A portico is essentially a covered, porch-like structure built to shelter the entryway to a house. Often, their primary purpose isn't protection from the elements as much as it is to give the house more architectural presence.

Tools & Materials ▸

Tape measure	Speed square	Nails	8d galvanized
Hammer drill with	Handsaw	4 × 4 metal post anchors	casing nails
⅜" masonry bit	Reciprocating saw	with standoffs	Roofing materials
Hammer	Straightedge	Deck screws	Exterior-grade caulk
Level	Nail set	⅜ × 4" lag screws	Quarter-round molding
Circular saw	Caulk gun	2 × 8 double	4d ringshank
Chalk line	Jigsaw	joist-hangers	siding nails
Drill with 1" spade bit	Paintbrush	Metal post caps	¾" cove molding
Ratchet wrench	⅜ × 3" masonry fasteners	8d siding nails	Wood putty
Torpedo level	10d joist-hanger nails	4d & 8d finish nails	Cedar scallops

Lumber (as needed)

2 × 4s (braces & stakes)
2 × 8s (ledger, beam members)
¼", ½" & ¾" exterior-grade plywood
1 × 10 finish lumber (beam wrap)

1 × 6s (beam brace, frieze boards, fascia, post collar wrap)
Trusses (order to size)
1 × 4 (truss braces, post wrap)
2 × 2 (nailing strips)

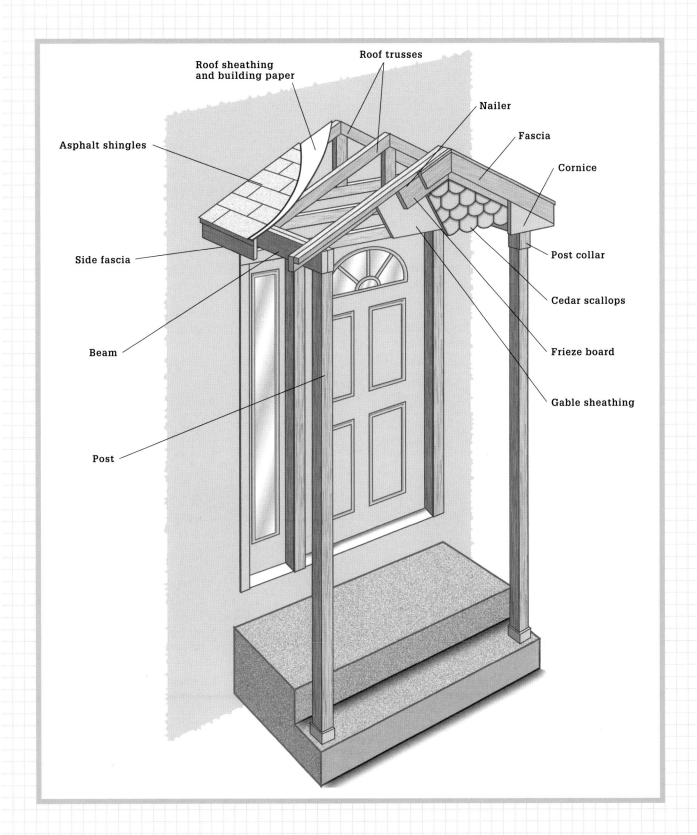

Roof sheathing and building paper

Roof trusses

Nailer

Fascia

Cornice

Asphalt shingles

Side fascia

Beam

Post

Post collar

Cedar scallops

Frieze board

Gable sheathing

How to Build a Portico

Install post anchors. Locate the post anchor so all the edges are at least 2" in from the edge of the concrete step or pad. Secure the post anchors' hardware with masonry anchors (inset) that are driven into the holes drilled in the concrete (use a hammer drill and a masonry bit). Some manufacturers suggest setting the anchors in epoxy glue in the hole for extra strength. Once the anchors are installed, you should have ¾" to 1" of the threaded bolt exposed. Secure the post anchor to the masonry anchor with a washer and nut.

Install the posts. Cut two 4 × 4 posts 6" longer than the planned post height *(Note: Some jurisdictions have a 6 × 6" minimum post size requirement.)*. Place the metal standoffs into each post anchor, then set a post onto each standoff. Tack each post in place with a single nail. Brace the posts with pairs of 2 × 4s attached to the stakes. Use a level to make sure the posts are plumb. Fully attach the posts to the post anchors with 10d joist-hanger nails.

Install the ledger. Mark an outline for the ledger at least 12" above the brickmold of the entrance. The outline should be ½" larger than the ledger on all four sides. Make reference marks at the midpoint on the ledger board and the ledger outline. Remove the siding in the outlined area. With centerpoints aligned, attach the ledger to each wall framing member with two counterbored lag screws (⅜ × 4").

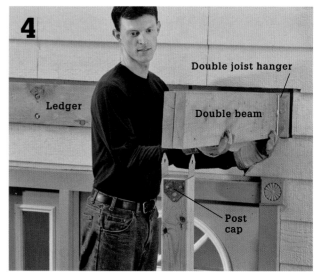

Install the beams. Mark the doubled beam locations at the ends of the ledger according to your plan. Fasten the double joist hangers to the ledger with 10d common nails at both beam locations. Fashion two doubled beams and temporarily rest each beam in its hanger. Clamp the free end to a post. Level the beam and then mark the post for trimming. Trim the post tops and install the post cap hardware. Position the beams and attach with 10d joist hanger nails.

5

Install the trusses. Position the first truss against the house, with the peak aligned on the project centerline. Make sure it is flush against the siding, then nail the rafter and bottom chords of the truss to the framing members using 20d common nails. Install the remaining trusses, working away from the house, by toenailing through the bottom chords and into the beams with 10d common nails. Nail the last truss flush with the ends of the beams. If the bottom chord of the first truss overhangs the beams, install the rest of the trusses with equal overhangs.

6

Install the roof and gable sheathing. Attach 2 × 2" nailing strips flush with the tops of the trusses. Install ¾" exterior-grade plywood roof sheathing to cover the trusses and nailing strips using 8d siding nails driven every 6" around the edges and every 12" in the field. The sheathing should be flush with the ends of the rafter tails. Also cut and install ¾" exterior-grade plywood to fit the triangular gable end.

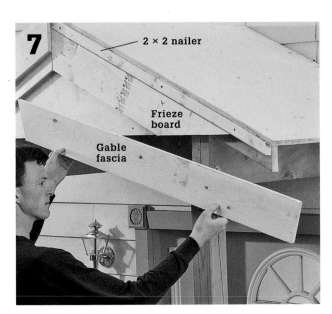

7

2 × 2 nailer

Frieze board

Gable fascia

Install the fascia. Cut 1 × 6 frieze boards to fit against the plywood gable sheathing, and attach the boards to the sheathing with 1¼" deck screws. Cut and install 1 × 6 gable fascia boards that extend several inches past the ends of the rafter tails. The top edges should be flush with the surface of the roof sheathing. Cut 1 × 8 side fascia boards to length, then rout a ⅜" groove 1" from the bottom edge to accept the soffit panels. Trim the ends of the gable fascia boards so they are flush with the ends of the side fascia boards.

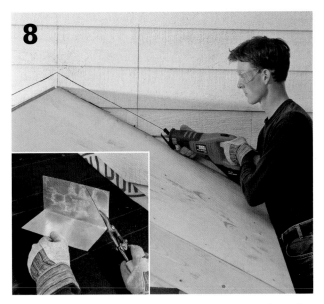

8

Prepare for step flashing. Trace cutting lines onto the wall siding 2" above the roof line. Cut the siding with a reciprocating saw held at a low angle and then remove the siding pieces. Try not to damage the sheathing. Fold the step flashing blanks longitudinally and trim the corners off two pieces so the vertical edge is upright (inset photo). Use these pieces at each end of the roof.

(continued)

Install the first row of shingles. Step flashing is essentially woven together with your shingles during the installation. Begin by installing a starter row of three-tab shingles upside-down at the eave (install building paper and drip edge first). Then, apply roofing cement to the back sides of a trimmed flashing piece and insert the flashing up under the siding, pressing the horizontal surface down against the shingle. Install a row of shingles with the tabs down, setting the shingle into a bed of roofing cement on the step flashing.

Finish roofing. Continue to shingle and flash the roof, maintaining a regular shingle pattern with a consistent exposed area on the shingle tabs. Make sure to stagger the shingle tabs in a regular pattern. Complete both sides of the roof, trimming the shingles at the gable end, and then cover the ridge with ridge cap shingles.

Wrap the beams and attach the post collars. Use finish-grade lumber to cover the beams and any metal hardware. Attach 1 × 10 boards to clad the sides of the beams. If necessary, add ½" plywood strips at the top and bottom of the beam. Use 1 × 4s to clad the bottoms of the beams. Create a 3" top collar where the posts meet the beam and a 1 × 10 end cap to cover the beam ends and the top collar. Add a 3" collar around the bottom of each post.

Wrap the ledger board. Measure the exposed ledger and cut a piece of finish lumber to size. If the ledger protrudes past the siding, cut a furring strip to cover the gap between the inside face of the ledger cover and the siding. Install the ledger cover with 8d finish nails.

Finish the cornice. For each end of the portico roof, cut a triangular piece of finish-grade lumber to make a cornice return. Test-fit the cornice pieces over the ends of the gable, then install with 8d finish nails driven into the ends of the beams, and 4d finish nails driven up through the ends of the cornice pieces and into the underside of the gable fascia. Set the nail heads and then caulk between the fascia boards and the cornice.

Install the soffits. Transfer the tops of the grooves in the side fascia board to the beam and attach 2 × 2 nailers just above that point. Measure from the back of the groove to the beam to find the required width of the soffit panel. Cut a piece of ⅜"-thick plywood to fit. Insert one edge of the soffit panel into the plow, then nail the other edge to the nailer with 4d finish nails. Add quarter-round molding at the joint between the soffit and the beam, or fill the gaps with exterior-grade caulk.

Install the ceiling. Cut ½" plywood or your chosen ceiling material to size. Cut the ceiling pieces so that any seams fall on the centers of the truss rafters. Use 4d ringshank siding nails to attach the plywood, spacing nails at 8 to 12" intervals. Install ¾" cove molding around the edges of the ceiling to cover the gaps. Miter the corners and attach with 4d finish nails. Set the nail heads slightly, and cover with wood putty. *Note: If installing wiring and an electrical box for ceiling lights, do it before installing the ceiling.*

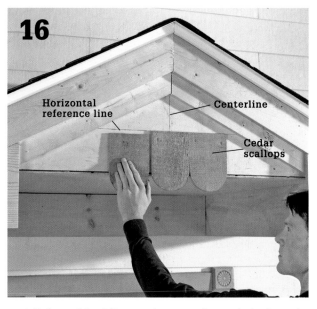

Horizontal reference line

Centerline

Cedar scallops

Install the gable siding. Mark a centerline and a horizontal reference line in the gable area. Starting at the centerline, align a piece of decorative gable siding (scallops seen here) with the intersecting reference lines, and fasten in place with a pair of 4d finish nails. Continue installing the trim. At the frieze boards, position the trim and mark the points where they intersect the frieze boards. Cut trim pieces to fit with a jigsaw. Stagger the pieces in a regular pattern. Paint or stain any exposed wood to match the house trim.

Screened-in Porches

If you have ever built a stud wall and repaired a window screen, you already have most of the skills needed for a screened-in project. A screen-in can be accomplished on many areas of a house or yard, including decks, patios, and gazebos. But by far the most popular area for a screen-in is the front porch. The quick and simple front porch screen-in demonstrated on the following pages is a good example of how to make outdoor living space more livable.

There are several strategies that can be employed for screening-in a porch. If you already have a basic framework of posts and rails, you can attach screen and trim directly to the framing, then add a screen door to complete the enclosure. If no suitable frame exists, you can build a simple 2 × 4 frame.

The traditional way to install screening is to staple it directly to the frame members then cover the staples with trim or to hold the screen in place with a decorative retaining strip. Another option is to use a screening kit, which yields a clean, finished look and drum-tight screens that are easier to repair than traditional staple-and-trim installations. A third method is to build individual screen frames to fit inside each opening in the porch framework. The main advantage with these methods is that you can easily remove the screens for the colder months of the year.

Tools & Materials ▸

Basic hand tools	Fiberglass insect
Saws	mesh screening
Staple gun	Screen retaining strips
Carpenter's level	Brass brads
Framing lumber	Screen door
Deck screws	

Screening in a porch is an inexpensive way to make your outdoor living space more comfortable.

Choosing a Screen Material ▸

Screening for porches, doors, and windows has performed the same primary function—keeping the bugs out—since it came into popular use in the late-1800s, but today's screening products can offer more than protection from insects. To help you select the right material for your project, here is a look at the most common types of screening and the specific properties of each.

FIBERGLASS

By far the most common type of screen used for porches, fiberglass mesh is inexpensive and offers good visibility due to minimal glare from sunlight. Fiberglass screen won't crease like metal screening, and its flexibility makes it the easiest type to work with. Its main drawbacks are that it stretches and tears more easily than most other screen types. Commonly available in black, silver gray, and charcoal; black tends to produce the least glare.

ALUMINUM

Aluminum is the other standard screen material and costs about a third more than fiberglass. It offers excellent visibility, but glare can be a problem, especially with bare (silver) metal screen. Aluminum screen is more rigid than fiberglass and thus a little harder to install, but it's also more durable, although it is prone to creasing during installation and to denting at any time. In coastal areas, aluminum will oxidize. Available in gray, black, and charcoal; black usually offers the best visibility.

PREMIUM METALS

For upscale jobs, screen is available in bronze, stainless steel, copper, and monel (a nickel-copper alloy). All of these are tough, long-lasting, and desired for their specific coloring and somewhat more elegant appearance over standard screening. Bronze, stainless steel, and monel hold up well in seaside climates.

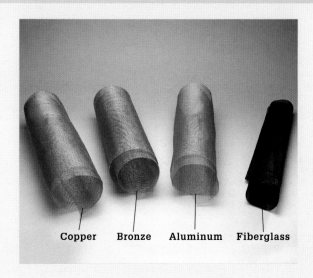

Copper   Bronze   Aluminum   Fiberglass

SUN CONTROL

For porches and sunrooms that tend to overheat in the summer, sun-blocking screen is available in a variety of types. The idea here is to keep out the bugs, along with most of the sun's heat, while letting light pass through to the interior of the space and still maintaining good exterior visibility. Some sun control screens can keep up to 90% of the sun's heat from getting inside.

PET-RESISTANT

Pet screening is many times stronger than standard mesh—perfect for owners of dogs, cats, small children, and other loveable but destructive creatures. It's more expensive (and affords less visibility) than standard screen, so you might choose to install pet screening only along the lower portion of screened walls, such as below a sturdy mid-rail or hand railing.

Understanding Screen Weave

Standard insect screening is made from woven strands of material. The tightness of the weave, or mesh size, is measured in the number of strands per inch. Standard mesh is 18 × 16, which has 18 strands per inch in one direction and 16 strands in the other direction. For large expanses of unsupported screen, you might consider using 18 × 14 mesh. This has slightly heavier strands, so the screen holds up better when stretched over large areas. If you live in a climate where tiny "no-see-um" bugs are a problem, you might need 20 × 20 mesh screen, which offers the best protection from teensy pests.

How to Screen in Porches

Outline the project area on the porch floor using a chalk line. The goal is to create the largest possible space not obstructed by beams, posts, railings, trim, or the ceiling. Check the corners of the outline with a framing square to make sure the chalk lines are square. Mark the door's rough opening—the door width plus 3" for the door frame and ½" for the door.

Attach 2 × 4 sole plates to the porch floor inside the outline using 3" deck screws driven at 12" intervals. Do not install sole plates in the door's rough opening. *Tip: Paint all of the wood parts for the screen-in before you install them.*

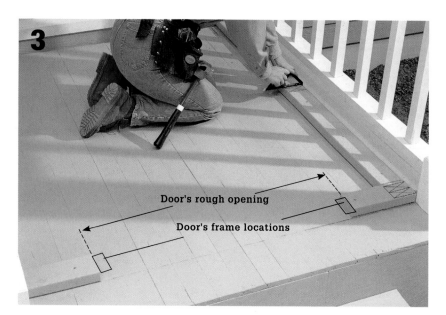

Door's rough opening

Door's frame locations

Mark stud and post locations on the sole plates. Start by marking 2 × 4 door frames at the sides of the door's rough opening—frames should rest on the floor, butted against sole plates. Mark the doubled 2 × 4 posts at the front corners of the project outline, and mark 2 × 4 end posts on the sole plates next to the wall of the house. Mark the 2 × 4 studs for screen supports, spaced at even intervals of 24" to 36", depending on the total distance spanned. Lay the 2 × 4 top plates (cut to match the sole plates) next to the sole plates, and copy post and stud marks onto the top plates. The top plate is not cut out for the door opening.

Using a straight 2 × 4 and a level, mark the locations for the top plates on the ceiling directly above the sole plates.

5

Attach the top plates to the ceiling with 3" deck screws driven into the rafters, if possible. Make sure the top plates are aligned directly above the sole plates, with the framing member marks also in alignment.

6

Cut the studs and posts to length, then position and install them at the marks on the top plates and the sole plates. Install by toenailing with 16d galvanized casing nails. When installing the 2 × 4 door frames, nail through the frames and into the ends of the sole plates.

Tip ▸

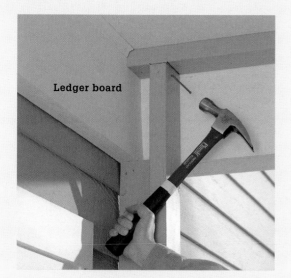

Ledger board

If the ledger board sticks out past the siding, work around it when installing the 2 × 4 end posts. One solution is to butt two 2 × 4s together so one fits between the floor and the ledger, with the edge against the wall. Toenail the other 2 × 4 into the top plate and sole plate, and nail it to the edge of the first 2 × 4.

7

Cut 2 × 4 spreaders to fit between the studs and the posts at the same height as the porch railing. Attach them with 16d casing nails. The spreaders prevent framing members from warping and provide a nailing surface for screen retaining strips.

(continued)

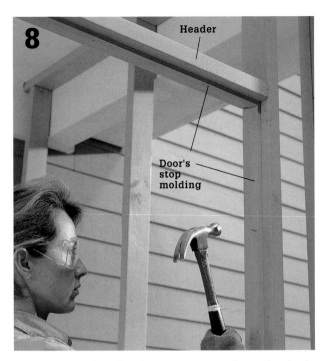

Header

Door's stop molding

Install a 2 × 4 door header to create a rough opening that is ¾" higher than the height of the screen door. Nail the doorstop molding to the inside faces of the door frames and header. The stop molding provides surfaces for the door to close against. It should be installed to create a recess the same thickness as the door, so that when it is closed, the door is flush with the outside edges of the door frame.

Attach the hinges to the door. Most screen doors are not prehung, so you will need to buy hinges separately. We used three 2½" door hinges. Install one hinge 12" from the top of the door, and another 12" from the bottom. Space the third evenly between them. Cut a mortise for each hinge into the edge of the door using a wood chisel, then attach the hinges with wood screws.

Set the door in the opening using ½"-thick spacers to hold it up off the floor. Outline the hinge plates onto the front edge of the door frame.

Cut mortises into the door frame at the hinge locations using a wood chisel. The mortises should be deep enough so the hinge plate will be flush with the surface of the wood. Attach the hinge plates to the mortises in the door and then hang the door in the opening.

Install the door hardware, including a door pull, a closer or spring, a wind chain, and a latch or lock if desired. Read the manufacturer's directions for each piece of hardware. *Option: Install a rubber door sweep on the bottom of the door.*

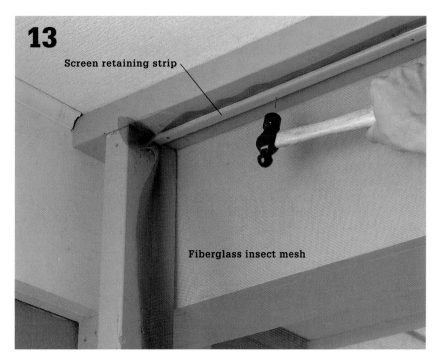

Screen retaining strip

Fiberglass insect mesh

Mark the centerlines along the inside faces of all studs, spreaders, and posts for reference when installing the screens. Using scissors, cut strips of screening so they are at least 4" wider and 4" longer than the opening in the framework where each screen will be installed. Begin attaching screens at the tops of the openings by securing them with wood screen retaining strips. Attach the retaining strips with brass brads spaced at 6 to 12" intervals.

With a helper, pull the screen down until it is taut. Use a retaining strip (cut to the width of the opening) to press the screen against the reference line. Attach the bottom retaining strip near the ends, then staple the screen at the sides, flush against the reference lines. Attach retaining strips at the sides of the opening.

Use a utility knife to trim excess screening at the edges of the retaining strips. Install screens in all of the remaining openings.

Under-deck Enclosure

Second-story walk-out decks can be a mixed blessing. On top, you have an open, sun-filled perch with a commanding view of the landscape. The space below the deck, however, is all too often a dark and chilly nook that is functionally unprotected from water runoff. As a result, an under-deck area often ends up as wasted space or becomes a holding area for seasonal storage items or the less desirable outdoor furniture.

But there's an easy way to reclaim all that convenient outdoor space—by installing a weatherizing ceiling system that captures runoff water from the deck above, leaving the area below dry enough to convert into a versatile outdoor room. You can even enclose the space to create a screened-in patio room.

The under-deck system featured in this project is designed for do-it-yourself installation. Its components are made to fit almost any standard deck and come in three sizes to accommodate different deck-joist spacing (for 12", 16", and 24" on-center spacing). Once the system is in place, the under-deck area is effectively "dried in", and you can begin adding amenities like overhead lighting, ceiling fans, and speakers to complete the outdoor room environment.

The system works by capturing water that falls through the decking above and channeling it to the outside edge of the deck. Depending on your plans, you can let the water fall from the ceiling panels along the deck's edge, or you can install a standard rain gutter and downspout to direct the water to a single exit point on the ground.

Tools & Materials ▸

4-ft. level	Under-deck
Chalk line	ceiling system
Caulking gun	Waterproof
Drill	acrylic caulk
Aviation snips	1" stainless
Hacksaw	steel screws
(for optional	Rain gutter system
rain gutter)	(optional)

Made of weather-resistant vinyl, this under-deck system creates an attractive, maintenance-free ceiling that keeps the space below dry throughout the seasons.

Design Tips

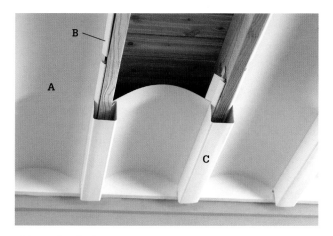

This under-deck system (see Resources, page 234) consists of four main parts: The joist rails mount to the deck joists and help secure the other components. The collector panels (A) span the joist cavity to capture water falling through the deck above. Water flows to the sides of the panels where it falls through gaps in the joist rails (B) and into the joist gutters (C) (for interior joists) and boundary gutters (for outer joists). The gutters carry the water to the outside edge of the deck.

For a finished look, paint the decking lumber that will be exposed after the system is installed. Typically, the lower portion of the ledger board (attached to the house) and the outer rim joist (at the outer edge of the deck) remain exposed.

Consider surrounding architectural elements when you select a system for sealing off the area below your deck. Here, the under-deck system is integrated with the deck and deck stairs both visually and functionally.

How to Install an Under-deck System

Check the undersides of several deck joists to make sure the structure is level. This is important for establishing the proper slope for effective water flow.

How bad is it? If your deck is not level, you must compensate for this when setting the ceiling slope. To determine the amount of correction that's needed, hold one end of the level against a joist and tilt the level until it reads perfectly level. Measure the distance from the joist to the free end of the level. Then, divide this measurement by the length of the level. For example, if the distance is ¼" and the level is 4 ft. long, the deck is out of level by ¹⁄₁₆" per foot.

To establish the slope for the ceiling system, mark the ends of the joists closest to the house: Measure up from the bottom 1" for every 10 ft. of joist length (or approximately ⅛" per ft.) and make a mark. Mark both sides of each intermediate joist and the inside faces of the outer joists.

Create each slope reference line using a chalk line: Hold one end of the chalk line at the mark made in Step 3, and hold the other end at the bottom edge of the joist where it meets the rim joist at the outside edge of the deck. Snap a reference line on all of the joists.

Install vinyl flashing along the ledger board in the joist cavities. Attach the flashing with 1" stainless steel screws. Caulk along the top edges of the flashing where it meets the ledger and both joists using quality, waterproof acrylic caulk. Also caulk the underside of the flashing for an extra layer of protection.

Begin installing the joist rails, starting 1" away from the ledger. Position each rail with its bottom edge on the chalk line, and fasten it to the joist at both ends with 1" stainless steel screws; then add one or two screws in between. Avoid over-driving the screws and deforming the rail; leaving a little room for movement is best.

Install the remaining rails on each joist face, leaving a 1½" (minimum) to 2" (maximum) gap between rails. Install rails along both sides of each interior joist and along the insides of each outside joist. Trim the final rail in each row as needed using aviation snips.

Measure the full length of each joist cavity, and cut a collector panel ¼" shorter than the cavity. This allows room for expansion of the panels. For narrower joist cavities, trim the panel to width following the manufacturer's sizing recommendations.

(continued)

Scribe and trim the collector panels for a tight fit against the ledger board. Hold a carpenter's pencil flat against the ledger, and move the pencil along the board to transfer its contours to the panel. Trim the panel along the scribed line.

Trim the corners of the collector panels as needed to accommodate joist hangers and other hardware. This may be necessary only at the house side of the joist cavity; at the outer end, the ¼" expansion gap should clear any hardware.

Trim panel here

Install the collector panels, starting at the house. With the textured side of the panel facing down, insert one side edge into the joist rails, and then push up gently on the opposite side until it fits into the opposing rails. When fully installed, the panels should be tight against the ledger and have a ¼" gap at the rim joist.

Prepare each joist gutter by cutting it ¼" shorter than the joist it will attach to (if the joists rest on a structural beam, see Variation, on page 104). On the house end of each gutter, trim the corners of the flanges at 45°. This helps the gutter fit tightly to the ledger.

13

Cut four or five ⅛" tabs into the bottom surface at the outside ends of the gutters. This helps promote the drainage of water over the edge of the gutter.

14

Caulk here

Attach self-adhesive foam weatherstrip (available from the manufacturer) at the home-end of each joist gutter. Run a bead of caulk along the foam strip to water-seal it to the gutter. The weather strip serves as a water dam.

15

Install each joist gutter by spreading its sides open slightly while pushing the gutter up onto the joist rails until it snaps into place. The gutter should fit snugly against the collector panels. The gutter's home-end should be tight against the ledger, with the ¼" expansion gap at the rim joist.

16

Prepare the boundary gutters following the same steps used for the joist gutters. Install each boundary gutter by slipping its long, outside flange behind the joist rails and pushing up until the gutter snaps into place. Install the boundary gutters working from the house side to the outer edge of the deck.

17

Run a bead of color-matched caulk along the joint where the collector panels meet the ledger board. This is for decorative purposes only and is not required to prevent water intrusion.

18

If collector panels are misshapen because the joist spacing is too tight, free the panel within the problem area, then trim about ⅛" from the side edge of the panel. Reset the panel in the rails. If necessary, trim the panel edge again in slight increments until the panel fits properly.

Working Around Beams ▸

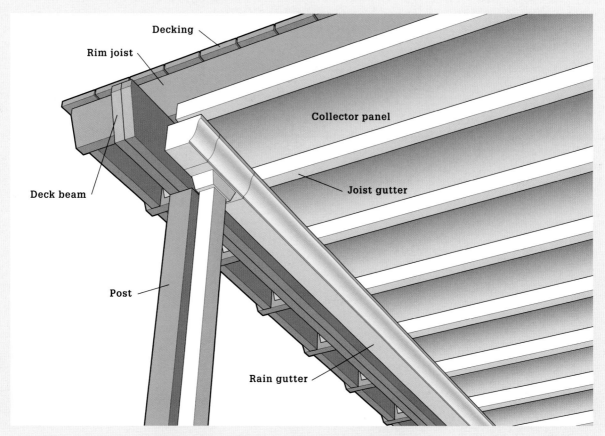

Decking

Rim joist

Collector panel

Deck beam

Joist gutter

Post

Rain gutter

For decks that have joists resting on top of a structural beam, stop the joist gutters and boundary gutters 1½" short of the beam. Install a standard rain gutter along the house-side of the beam to catch the water as it exits the system gutters (see pages 239 to 241). (On the opposite side of the beam, begin new runs of joist gutters that are tight against the beam and stop ¼" short of the rim joist. The joist rails and collector panels should clear the beam and can be installed as usual.) Or, you can simply leave the overhang area alone if you do not need water runoff protection below it.

Runoff Gutters

A basic gutter system for a square or rectangular deck includes a straight run of gutter channel with a downspout at one end. Prefabricated vinyl or aluminum gutter parts are ideal for this application. Gutter channels are commonly available in 10-ft. and 20-ft. lengths, so you might be able to use a single channel without seams. Otherwise, you can join sections of channel with special connectors. Shop around for the best type of hanger for your situation. If there's limited backing to support the back side of the channel or to fasten into, you may have to use strap-type hangers that can be secured to framing above the gutter.

Runoff gutters are installed at the ends of the under-deck channels to capture runoff water and redirect it away from the enclosed area through downspouts.

How to Install an Under-deck Runoff Gutter

1

Snap a chalk line onto the beam or other supporting surface to establish the slope of the main gutter run. The line will correspond to the top edge of the gutter channel. The ideal slope is 1/16" per foot. For example, with a 16-ft.-long gutter, the beginning is 1" higher than the end. The downspout should be located just inside the low end of the gutter channel. Mark the beam at both ends to create the desired slope, then snap a chalk line between the marks. The high end of the gutter should be just below the boundary gutter in the ceiling system.

(continued)

2

Install a downspout outlet near the end of the gutter run so the top of the gutter is flush with the slope line. If you plan to enclose the area under the deck, choose an inconspicuous location for the downspout, away from traffic areas.

3

Install hanger clips (depending on the type of hangers or support clips you use, it is often best to install them before installing the gutter channel). Attach a hanger every 24" so the top of the gutter will hang flush with the slope line.

Tip ▶

Gutters come in several material types, including PVC, enameled steel and copper. In most cases you should try to match the surrounding trim materials, but using a more decorative material for contrast can be effective.

4

Cut sections of gutter channel to size using a hacksaw. Attach an end cap to the beginning of the main run, then fit the channel into the downspout outlet (allowing for expansion, if necessary) and secure the gutter in place.

5

Join sections of channel together, if necessary, for long runs using connectors. Install a short section of channel with an end cap on the opposite side of the downspout outlet. Paint the area where the downspout will be installed if it is unpainted.

6

Hanger

Cut the downspout piping to length and fasten an elbow fitting to its bottom end. Attach the downspout to the downspout outlet, then secure the downspout to a post or other vertical support using hangers (inset).

7

Cut a drainpipe to run from the downspout elbow to a convenient drainage point. Position the pipe so it directs water away from the house and any traffic areas. Attach the pipe to the downspout elbow. Add a splash block, if desired.

Routing Drainpipes ▶

You may have to get a little creative when routing the downspout drain in an enclosed porch or patio. Shown here, two elbows allow for a 90° turn of the drainpipe.

Installing a Porch Screen Kit

A screening system is an ingeniously simple and effective way to enclose a porch with minimal time and effort. A basic system includes three main components: a base channel that mounts directly to the porch posts, railings, and other framing members; the screening (and spline, if applicable); and a trim cap that snaps in place over the base channel to cover the screen edges and add a finished look to the installation. The base and cap pieces are made to go together, but the screen and spline are purchased separately. Be sure to follow the system manufacturer's specifications for screen type and spline size. Screen systems typically are compatible with fiberglass and aluminum screen materials (see page 93).

With the system shown in this project, each piece of screen is secured into the base channels using standard vinyl or rubber spline and a spline roller. The screen goes up quickly and easily after a little practice, and it doesn't have to be perfectly tight right away; when the cap pieces are snapped on, they add tension to the screening,

pulling it tight from all sides of the opening. This does a good job of eliminating the unsightly sag that occurs all too quickly with standard stapled-up screening. Replacing screen sections also is much easier with a screen system: Just remove the surrounding cap pieces, pull out the spline, and install a new piece of screen.

Tools & Materials ▸

Hammer	Screen system
Pry bar	components
Pruning sheers or	1" corrosion-resistant
aviation snips	screws
Drill	Screening
Spline roller	Spline cord
Utility knife	2 × 4 lumber or
Rubber mallet	composite equivalent

Screen systems are quick, easy products for screening in porches and other areas, such as the under-deck space seen here. They are commonly available at home centers and hardware stores and through Internet sites. Screen Tight, the system shown here, is made with UV-resistant PVC and is available with trim colors of white, gray, beige, and brown (see Resources, page 234).

Cladding Posts ▸

With their textures and grain, plain wood posts are right at home in many parts of many homes. But when you combine them with gleaming new white vinyl-based products; they can look a little rough. One way to make your porch posts blend better when you're installing under-deck or screening systems is to clad them and paint them to match. Traditionally, clear dimensional lumber is used for the cladding. But to get seamless results; this often means you need to cut complicated dado-rabbet joints that run all the way from top to bottom at each corner. Then, you need to sand thoroughly and apply several coats of paint. An easier option for making all of your screen porch parts match is to clad posts with one-piece PVC post cladding (see Resources, page 234). The product shown here is designed to fit around a 6 × 6" post. On the interior surface it is kerfed but the exterior vinyl surface is solid. This way, it can be bent around corners crisply and seamlessly.

Vinyl cladding can be wrapped around wood posts seamlessly.

Spline-based screening systems are available at home centers and hardware stores and through many websites. Screen Tight, the system shown here (see Resources, page 234), is made with UV-resistant PVC and is available with trim colors of white, gray, beige, and brown. Parts of the system include: stretchable spline cord (A); spline roller (B); adhesive for bonding rigid vinyl (C); storm door handles (D); storm door hinges (E); 1" corrosion-resistant screws (F); screw-eye door latch (G); deck screws (H); decorative white-cap screws (I); track cap (J); track base (K); composite 2 × 4 (L); fiberglass screening (M).

How to Create Screened Rooms with a Spline Kit

Begin installing the track backers that frame the openings you will be screening. You may use pressure-treated 2 × 4s or 2 × 2s. For a long-lasting and low-maintenance framework, we used composite 2 × 4-sized backers that came with the screen system materials. These products are quite new and are not rated for structural use. Attach the backers to the inside faces of the posts, centered, using exterior construction adhesive and 3½" deck screws.

Secure sole plates to the patio or porch floor using construction adhesive and appropriate mechanical fasteners (use concrete anchors for concrete, stone or paver patios and use deck screws for wood and nonwood decking).

Attach cap plates to the beam or joist at the top of installation area, leaving 1½" between plates to create recesses for the vertical backers.

Install the vertical track backer members with the top ends fitted in the gaps you left in the cap plate. Make sure the vertical members are plumb and then drive deck screws toenail style through the members and into the sole plate. Also drive screws up at angles through the vertical members and into the beam or joist at the top of the area. Drill pilot holes.

5

Install the door header and the horizontal track backers using adhesive and deck screws. Locate the horizontal members 36 to 42" above the ground.

6

Cut a base channel to length for each vertical member in the porch frame. At the tops of the posts, hold the base channel back to allow room for the horizontal channels, if applicable (see step 11 photo). This results in less cutting of the cap trim later. Cut the channels using pruning shears, aviation snips, or a power miter saw.

7

Fasten the vertical channel pieces to the framing with 1" corrosion-resistant screws. Drive a screw into each predrilled hole in the channel, then add a screw 2" from each end. Drive each screw in snugly but not so far that it warps the channel.

8

Cut the horizontal base channels to length and install them with screws. The butted joints where the horizontal channels meet the verticals don't have to be precise or tight-fitting.

(continued)

Begin installing the screen by positioning a full piece of screening over an opening so it overlaps several inches on all sides. Secure the screen into the horizontal base channel at one of the top corners using spline. You can plan to run the spline around the corners or cut it off at the ends as needed.

Embed the spline at the starting point, where it should fit fully into the groove of the base channel. Use a spline roller. Then, using one hand to pull the screen taut, press the spline into place to secure the screen along the top of the opening.

Secure the screen along both sides, then along the bottom using the same technique as for the top. When you're finished, the screen should be flat and reasonably tight, with no sagging or wrinkling. If you make a mistake or the screen won't cooperate, simply remove the spline and start over.

Trim off the excess screening with a sharp utility knife. Fiberglass screen cuts very easily, so control the knife carefully at all times. Repeat steps as needed to screen-in the remaining openings.

Install the trim caps over the base channels, starting with the vertical pieces. Working from the bottom up, center the cap over the base, then tap it into place using a rubber mallet. *Tip: If you have a continuous horizontal band along the top of the screening, install those trim pieces before capping the verticals.*

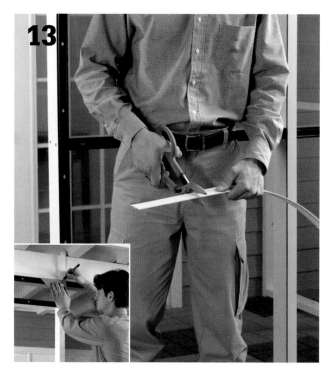

Cut the cap pieces to length as you install them. Mark cutting lines with a pencil, and make the cuts with pruning shears or snips. If desired, use a square to mark a straight cutting line across the face or backside of the trim cap (inset).

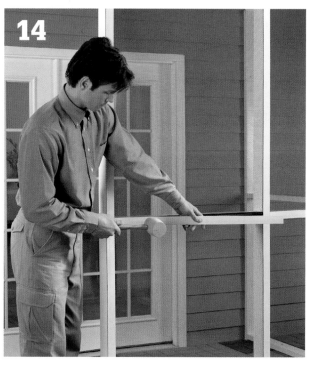

Install the horizontal pieces once the vertical cap pieces are in place, using the same techniques. Butt the horizontals tight against the verticals to start each piece, and then trim it to length as you approach the opposite end.

Complete the screening project by installing a screen door. A low-maintenance vinyl door provides a good match with the finish of the vinyl trim cap, but a traditional painted wood door is also appropriate. See pages 115 to 117 for door installation steps.

Option: To protect the screening from being damaged by pets, kids, or other causes, make lattice frames and install them in the framed areas.

Screen Doors

The slamming of a screen door is one of the most evocative sounds of summer. But nostalgia isn't the only reason traditional swinging doors remain such a popular choice for screened porches. These simple doors are also inexpensive, convenient to use, and easy to install. And those made with newer materials, such as vinyl, are virtually maintenance-free. Of course, you can still find plenty of screen doors that are made from solid wood if you are one of those who yearn for just the right timbre in their slam.

This project shows the basic steps for installing a standard screen door, with tips for working with both vinyl and wood products. Hanging a door is pretty straightforward; what differences there are among installations usually result from the type of hardware used, namely, whether the hinges are designed to be surface-mounted or to be set into mortises for a flush installation. You can get away with surface-mounting most types of hinges, but with mortised hinges, the job looks much more professional if you spend the time to cut mortises.

Tools & Materials ▸

Circular saw
Straightedge
  and clamps
Utility knife
Sandpaper
Wood chisel
  and router
  (optional) for
  mortised hinges
Drill and bits
Screen door

Tapered wood shims
Corrosion-resistant
  hinges (3)
  with screws
Doorstop molding
Finish nails
Corrosion-resistant
  door handles
  and hardware
  (as desired)

Screen doors are commonly available made from wood, vinyl, and aluminum. Standard widths are 30", 32", and 36" with a standard height of 80". Door thickness is typically 1" to 1¼". Wood and some vinyl doors can be trimmed to fit an opening and can be mortised for hinges. Metal doors cannot be cut, but they may come with size-adjustment features.

How to Install a Porch Screen Door

Measure the door opening. The new screen door should be ¼" to ⅜" narrower and ¼" to ½" shorter than the opening. Plan to trim the door, if necessary, for proper clearance. Some vinyl doors should not be cut, while others may be cut only a limited amount. If the door is vinyl, check with the manufacturer:

To trim the height of a door, mark the cutting line, then clamp a straightedge to the door to guide your circular saw for a straight cut. For wood doors, score deeply along the cutting line with a utility knife before setting up the straightedge; this prevents splintering on the top side when cutting across the grain.

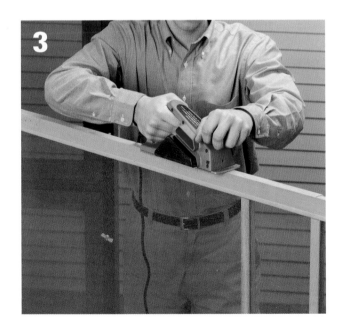

To trim the width of a door, it's usually best to remove material from the hinge side, which is less visible. Mark a full-length cutting line, and make the cut with a circular saw. Or, you can use a power hand planer to trim off material from the edge. Use sandpaper or a file to round-over the cut side (and bottom, if applicable) edges to match the uncut edges and to prevent splinters.

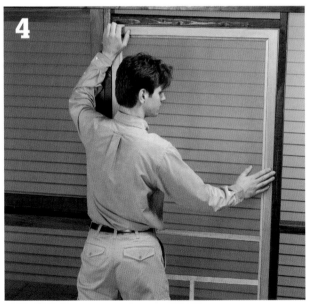

Test-fit the door in the opening using wood shims along the bottom to raise the door to the right heights. Center the door from side to side; the reveal here should be about ⅛" on each side.

(continued)

Mount the hinges to the door using screws driven into pilot holes (three hinges is preferable, but two will work for most doors). Position the top hinge about 7" from the top of the door, the bottom hinge about 10" from the bottom, and the middle hinge halfway between the other two. See the next page for how to mortise standard hinges.

Install the door. Set the door into the opening using shims at the sides to establish equal reveals. For surface-mount hinges, mark and drill pilot holes, then screw the hinges to the side jamb or post to hang the door. For mortised hinges, transfer the hinge locations to the jamb, cut mortises for the hinges, then hang the door.

Install doorstop molding around the sides and top of the door opening using galvanized finish nails if your screen door is not prehung. Position the stops so the outer door face is flush with the outer jamb edges, trim, or door posts, as applicable. Install the stop along the top of the opening first, then along the sides.

Add door handles, latches, and closer hardware as desired, following the manufacturer's instructions. A closer is a good idea to prevent the door from being left open and admitting insects. Closers come in a range of types, including spring-loaded hinges, hydraulic pistons, and old-fashioned extension springs. Most also have a stop chain that prevents the door from blowing all the way open.

How to Cut Hinge Mortises

Trace the hinge leaf outline. If your hinges have a removable pin, separate the leaves first. Some hinge barrels are fused on the top and bottom so you cannot remove the pin. Hold a leaf against the door edge at the marked position, and then carefully score around the leaf with a sharp utility knife. Make a second scoring pass, cutting to a depth equal to the thickness of the leaf.

Make a series of cuts across the mortise area using a chisel. The cut depth should match the thickness of the hinge leaf. Chip away the waste material, holding the chisel at a low angle, to create a smooth, level mortise (inset). Test-fit the hinge leaf and remove more material as needed so the leaf is flush with the door edge.

Variation: Mortise with a Router

To cut mortises with a router or spiral-cut saw, score around the hinge leaf as described above. Use a straight router bit that cuts a flat bottom, and set the bit depth to match the thickness of the hinge leaf (make some test cuts on scrap wood to find the precise depth). Rout out the mortise freehand, staying about ⅛" inside of the score line. To prevent mistakes, make the perimeter cut first, then remove the interior material (left). When the routing is done, clean up the edges of the mortise with a chisel (right).

Building Removable Screens ▶

Screening-in a porch with custom-built screened frames initially takes more time and effort than applying screen directly to the porch framing. But frames come with a couple of key advantages. First, you can easily remove the screens during the cold season for unobstructed views from the house and to minimize wear and tear on the screens. And second, it's usually much easier to install and repair screens with removable frames than with a screen-in-place system, especially a staple-up systems.

You can build screen frames almost any way you like and you can even get a little creative. Following are some examples of standard frame construction and simple ways to attach screening, as well as ideas for installing the screens into the porch's framed openings. For an overview of screen materials, see page 93.

Be sure to use good, straight lumber for the frame stock. Shop around at local lumberyards to find the material that best meets your needs. The stock should be at least

Removable screens keep bugs out when the porch is in use, and they can be stored safely when not in use.

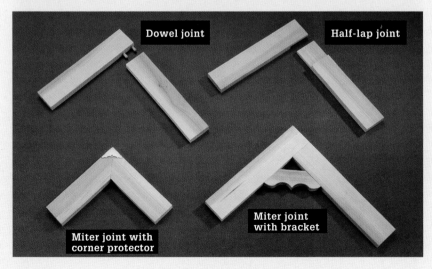

Dowel joint

Half-lap joint

Miter joint with bracket

Miter joint with corner protector

Reinforce frame corners with hardware or by using common woodworking joinery methods.

1" thick for strength. When it comes to sizing the frames, you'll build each to fit a specific opening, of course, but keep in mind that smaller screened areas are less prone to stretching and bulging over time. For this reason, professional glaziers often recommend limiting screen size to a maximum of 42 × 60". If an opening is larger than that, consider adding a crosspiece or mid-rail to the frame, thus creating two screened sections within a single frame unit.

BUILDING THE FRAME

Screen frames are often built with simple butt joints reinforced with glued dowels or metal brackets. Other woodworking joints are also appropriate, including mortise-and-tenon, half-lap, and mitered joints. In general, choose the strongest joint you can make with the tools (and skills) you have available. Be sure to mill rabbets and/or spline grooves into the pieces before assembling the frame.

ATTACHING SCREEN

Screening typically is fastened to frames either with staples spaced about 2" apart or with rubber or vinyl spline cord pressed into a groove. Cut these grooves with a circular saw using a blade that creates a snug fit for the spline. It always looks best to cover staples or spline with some kind of trim. The trim can fit into a rabbet (cut with a router or on a table saw) so it's flush with the frame, or you can simply nail or screw the trim to the surface of the frame pieces.

INSTALLING SCREEN FRAMES

Screens are installed into porch openings with wood stops on one or both sides of the screen frames. You can use any style of trim but 1 × 1 (¾" × ¾") stop material is most common. Install the stops along all four sides of each opening, sandwiching the screen frame in between. To remove the screens, unscrew or pry off the stops on one side. As an alternative (and the easiest way to remove screens), install only the outer stops so that the insides of the screen frames are flush with the porch framing, then hold the screens in place with butterfly clips or turn buttons.

Screening can be attached with staples or with spline cord. Retainer strips conceal the fasteners.

Use clips or turn buttons to secure frames against stops that are attached to the porch framing.

Patio Shelter

If you like the openness and plentiful light of a patio but want more protection from rain and strong winds, this stylish, contemporary patio shelter may be just what you're looking for. Designed as a cross between an open-air arbor or pergola and an enclosed three-season porch, this patio structure has clear glazing panels on its roof and sides, allowing plenty of sunlight through while buffering the elements and even blocking harmful UV rays.

The roof of the patio shelter is framed with closely spaced 2 × 4 rafters to create the same light-filtering effects of a slatted arbor roof. The rafters are supported by a doubled-up 2 × 10 beam and 4 × 6 timber posts. Because the shelter is attached to the house, the posts are set on top of concrete foundation piers, or footings, that extend below the frost line. This prevents any shifting of the structure in areas where the ground freezes in winter.

The patio shelter's side panels cut down on wind while providing a degree of privacy screening. Their simple construction means you can easily alter the dimensions or locations of the panels to suit your own plans. In the project shown, each side has two glazing panels with a 3½" space in between, for airflow. If desired, you can use a single sheet of glazing across the entire side section. The glazing is held in place with wood strips and screws so they can be removed for seasonal cleaning.

Slats of white oak sandwich clear polycarbonate panels to create walls that block the wind without blocking light and views.

Building against a solid wall and not in front of a patio door makes the space inside this contemporary shelter much more usable. The corrugated roof panels (see Resources, page 234) made of clear polycarbonate allow light to enter while keeping the elements out.

Patio Shelter

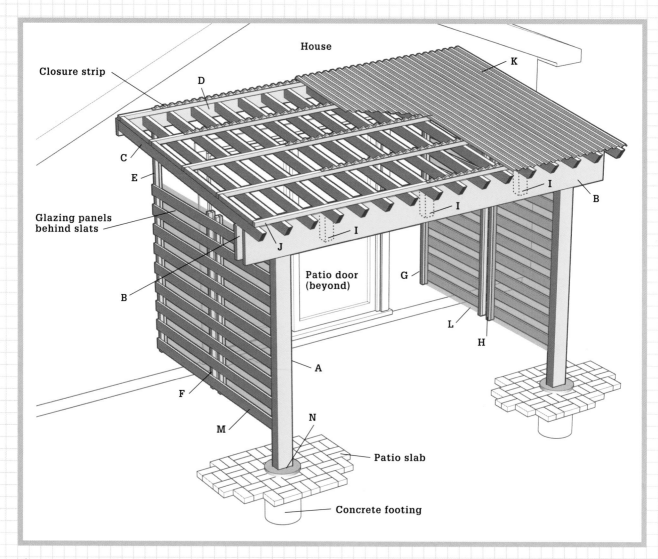

Closure strip

House

Glazing panels behind slats

Patio door (beyond)

Patio slab

Concrete footing

Plan your own patio shelter based on the requirements set by the local building code. Your city's building department or a qualified building professional can help you with the critical structural specifications, such as the size and depth of the concrete post footings, the sizing of beam members, and the overall roof construction. The building department will help make sure your shelter is suitable for the local weather conditions (particularly wind and snow loads).

Cutting List

Key	Part	No.	Size	Material
A	Post	2	3½ × 5½ × 144"	4 × 6 treated pine
B	Beam member	2	1½ × 9¼ × 120"*	2 × 10 treated pine
C	Rafter	16	1½ × 3½ × 120"*	2 × 4 pine
D	Ledger	1	1½ × 5½ × 144"	2 × 6 treated pine
E	Back post	2	1½ × 1½ × 96"*	2 × 2 pine
F	Slat cleat	4	1½ × 1½ × 60"	2 × 2 pine
G	Back post cap	2	¾ × 1½ × 96"*	1 × 2 pine

Key	Part	No.	Size	Material
H	Slat cleat cap	4	¾ × 1½ × 60"	1 × 2 pine
I	Beam blocks	3	3½ × 3½ × 8"	4 × 4 pine
J	Purlin	14	1½ × 1½ × 120"	2 × 2 pine
K	Roof panel	6	¼ × 26 × 96"	Corrugated polycarbonate
L	Side panel	4	¼ × 36 × 58"	Clear polycarbonate
M	Slat	18	¾ × 3½ × 80"*	White oak
N	Post base	2	1½ × 3½ × 3½	

*Size listed is prior to final trimming

Tools & Materials

Chalk line
4-ft. level
Plumb bob
Mason's string
Digging tools
Concrete mixing tools
Circular saw
Ratchet wrench
Line level
Reciprocating saw or handsaw
Drill
Finish application tools
Gravel
12"-dia. concrete tube forms
Concrete mix
⅝"-dia. J-bolts
⅜ × 4" corrosion resistant lag screws
Flashing

Silicone caulk
Corrosion-resistant metal post bases and hardware
Lumber
Corrosion-resistant 16d and 8d common nails
½"-dia. corrosion-resistant lag bolts and washers
Exterior wood glue or construction adhesive
Corrosion-resistant framing anchors (for rafters)
1½" and 3" deck screws
Polycarbonate roofing panels
Clear polycarbonate panels
Closure strips
Roofing screws with EPDM washers
Roofing adhesive/sealant
Wood finishing materials
Neoprene weatherstripping
Scrap lumber
Dark exterior wood stain

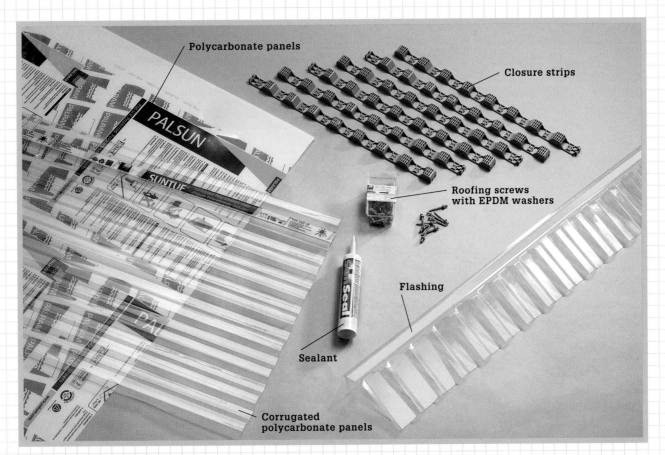

The roofing and side glazing panels of the patio shelter are made with tough polycarbonate materials. The corrugated roofing panels allow up to 90% light transmission while blocking virtually 100 percent of harmful UV rays. The flat side panels offer the transparency of glass but are lighter and much stronger than glass. Also shown is: wall flashing designed to be tucked under siding; closure strips that fit between the 2 × 2 purlins and the corrugated roof panels; self-sealing screws and polycarbonate caulk. For more information on these products, see Resources, page 234.

How to Build a Patio Shelter

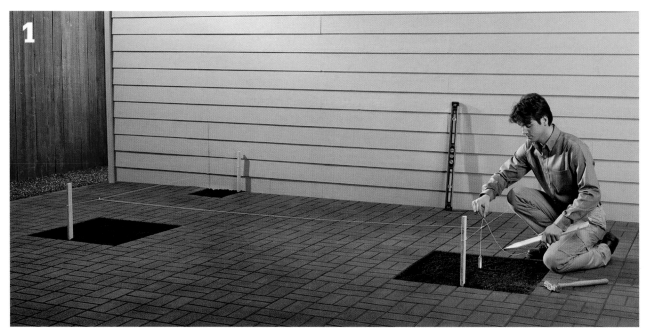

Mark the layout for the ledger board on the house wall. Lay out the post footing locations in the patio area. To mark the cutout for the ledger board, include the width of the ledger board, plus the height of the roofing, plus 1½" for the flashing. The length of the cutout should be 1" longer than the length of the ledger board (12 ft. as shown). Plumb down from the ends of the ledger, then measure in to mark the locations of the post centers. At each of these points, run a perpendicular string line from the house out to about 2 ft. beyond the post locations. Set up a third string line, perpendicular to the first two, to mark the centers of the posts. Plumb down from the string line intersections and mark the post centers on the ground with stakes.

Dig a hole for a concrete tube form at each post location following the local building code for the footing depth (plus 6" for gravel). Add 6" of gravel and tamp it down. Position the tube forms so they are plumb and extend at least 2" above the ground. Backfill around them with soil and compact thoroughly.

Fill the tube forms with concrete and screed it level with the tops of the forms. At each post-center location, embed a J-bolt into the wet concrete so it extends the recommended distance above the top of the form. Let the concrete cure.

4

Cut out the house siding for the ledger board using a circular saw. Cut only through the siding, leaving the wall sheathing intact. *(Note: If the sheathing is fiberboard instead of plywood, you may have to remove the fiberboard; consult your local building department.)* Replace any damaged building paper covering the sheathing.

5

Stain the wood parts before you begin installing the shelter closure strips and panels. We used a black, semitransparent deck and siding stain.

6

Apply a protective finish to the wood slats as desired. We used a semitransparent deck stain.

(continued)

7

Install the ledger. First, slip corrugated roof flashing or metal roof flashing behind the siding above the ledger cutout so the vertical flange extends at least 3" above the bottom of the siding. Cut the ledger board to length. Fasten the ledger to the wall using ⅜ × 4" lag screws driven through counterbored pilot holes at each wall-stud location. Seal over the screw heads and counterbores with silicone caulk.

8

Anchor the post bases to the concrete footing, securing them with the base manufacturer's recommended hardware. Make sure the bases are aligned with each other and are perpendicular to the house wall.

9

Cut off the bottom ends of the posts so they are perfectly square. Set each post in its base and hold it plumb. Fasten the post to the base using the manufacturer's recommended fasteners. Brace the posts with temporary bracing. *Note: You will cut the posts to length in a later step.*

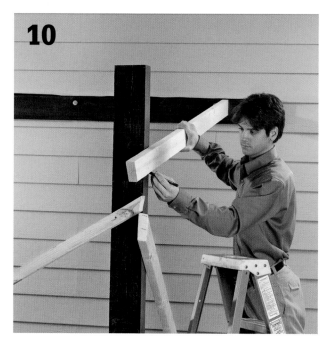

Cut a pattern rafter from 2 x 4 lumber using the desired roof slope to find the angle cut for the top end. Angle the bottom end as desired for decorative effect. Set the rafter in position so its top end is even with the top of the ledger and its bottom end passes along the side of a post. Mark along the bottom edge of the rafter onto the post. Repeat to mark the other post. Use a string and line level to make sure the post marks are level with each other.

Cut the inner beam member to length from 2 x 10 lumber, then bevel the top edge to follow the roof slope. Position the board so its top edge is on the post markings and it overhangs the posts equally at both ends (12" of overhang is shown). Tack the board in place with 16d nails.

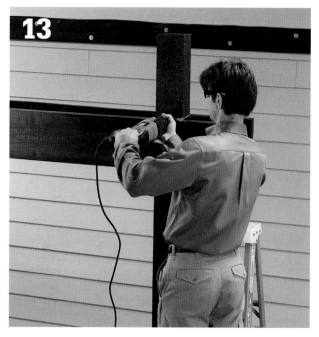

Cut the outer beam member to length from 2 × 10 lumber. Bevel the top edge following the roof slope, and remove enough material so that the bottom edges of the two beam members will be level with each other. Tack the member in place with nails.

Anchor the beam members together and to the posts with pairs of ½"-dia. lag bolts and washers. Cut the posts off flush with the tops of the beam members using a handsaw or reciprocating saw.

(continued)

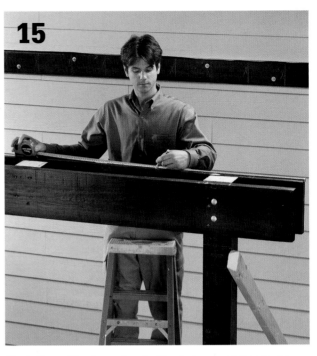

Trim the cutoff post pieces to length and use them as blocking between the beam members. Position the blocks evenly spaced between the posts and fasten them to both beam members with glue and 16d nails. *Note: Diagonal bracing between the posts and beam may be recommended or required in some areas; consult your local building department.*

Mark the rafter layout onto the ledger and beam. As shown here, the rafters are spaced 9½" apart on center. The two outer rafters should be flush with the ends of the ledger and beam.

Install metal framing anchors onto the ledger for securing the top rafter ends using the anchor manufacturer's recommended fasteners. Use the pattern rafter or a block to position the anchors so the rafters will be flush with the top of the ledger.

17

Use the pattern rafter to mark the remaining rafters and then cut them. Install the rafters one at a time. Fasten the top ends to the metal anchor using the recommended fasteners. Fasten the bottom ends to both beam members by toenailing one 8d nail through each rafter side and into the beam member.

18

Install the 2 x 2 purlins perpendicular to the rafters using 3" deck screws. Position the first purlin a few inches from the bottom ends of the rafters. Space the remaining purlins 24" on center. The ends of the purlins should be flush with the outside faces of the outer rafters.

19

Add 2 x 2 blocking between the purlins along the outer rafters, and fasten them with 3" deck screws. This blocking will support the vertical closure strips for the roof panels.

20

Starting at one side of the roof, install the roof panel closure strips over the purlins using the manufacturer's recommended fasteners. Begin every run of strips from the same side of the roof, so the ridges in the strips will be aligned.

(continued)

21

Add vertical closure strips over the 2 × 2 purlin blocking to fill in between the horizontal strips.

22

Position the first roofing panel along one side edge of the roof. The inside edge of the panel should fall over a rafter. If necessary, trim the panel to length or width following the manufacturer's recommendations.

23

Drill pilot holes, and fasten the first panel to the closure strips with the recommended type of screw and rubber washer. Fasten the panel at the peak (top) of every other corrugation. Drive the screws down carefully, stopping when the washer contacts the panel but is not compressed. This allows for thermal expansion of the panel.

24

Apply a bead of the recommended adhesive/sealant (usually supplied by the panel manufacturer) along the last trough of the roofing panel. Set the second panel into place, overlapping the last troughs on both panels. Fasten the second panel. Install the remaining panels using the same procedure. Caulk the seam between the roof panels and the roof flashing.

If you do not have wall flashing designed to work with the roof profile, place closure strips upside down onto the roof panels and run another bead of adhesive/sealant over the tops of the strips. Work the flashing down and embed it into the sealant. Seal along all exposed edges of the ledger with silicone caulk.

To create channels for the side glazing panels, mill a rabbet into each of the eight vertical 2 × 2 cleats. Consult the glazing manufacturer for the recommended channel size, making sure to provide space for thermal expansion of the panels. Mill the rabbets using a table saw, router, or circular saw. Stop the rabbets so the bottom edges of the panels will be even with, or slightly above, the bottom edge of the lowest side slat.

Position a cleat on each post at the desired height, with the cleat centered from side to side on the post. The rabbeted corner should face inside the shelter. Fasten the cleats to the posts with 3" deck screws. Fasten two more cleats to the house wall so they are aligned and level with the post cleats.

Cut the side slats to length to fit between the posts and the house wall. Mark the slat layouts onto the outside faces of the cleats, and install the slats with 1½" deck screws or exterior trim-head screws. Space the slats 3½" apart or as desired.

(continued)

28

Fasten the middle cleats to the slats on each side, leaving about 3½" of space between the cleats (or as desired). The cleats should overhang the top and bottom slats by 1½" (or as desired).

Tip ▶

Used for the decorative accent slats on this patio shelter, white oak is a traditional exterior wood that was employed for boatbuilding as well as outdoor furnishings. Although it requires no finishing, we coated the white oak with a dark, penetrating wood stain to bring out the grain.

29

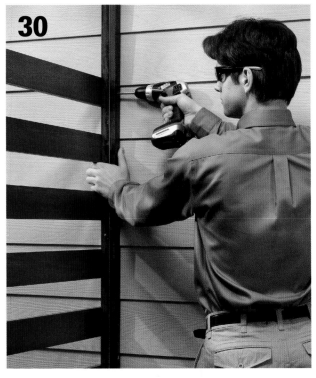

30

Cut the cap strips for the glazing panels from 1 × 2 material (or rip down strips from the 1 × 4 slat material). Position each cap over a cleat and drill evenly spaced pilot holes through the cap and into the cleat. Make sure the holes go into the solid (non-rabbeted) portion of the cleat. Drill counterbores, too (left). Drive screws to attach the post caps (right).

Option: Add a 2 × 4 decorative cap on the outside face of each post. Center the cap side-to-side on the post and fasten it with 16d casing nails.

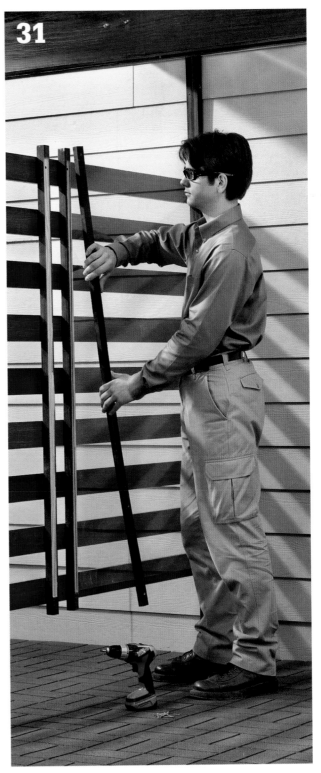

Trim the side glazing panels to size following the manufacturer's directions. Apply neoprene or EPDM stripping or packing to the side edges of the panels. Fit each panel into its cleat frame, cover the glazing edges with the 1 × 2 caps, and secure the caps with 1½" deck screws. *Note: If the glazing comes with a protective film, remove the film during this step as appropriate and make sure the panel is oriented for full UV protection.*

Patio Enclosures

A patio enclosure is any structure built around a patio to completely block out wind and rain. Typically, they are unheated and uninsulated, and electrical access is limited to exterior receptacles on the walls of the house.

The project shown on the following pages is a typical patio enclosure project. It is likely that your enclosure project will differ to some degree from the project shown here. But whatever the design of your own project, read this information carefully to gain a better understanding of the challenges you will encounter and to learn how those challenges can be addressed.

Be sure to check with your local building inspector before you begin the project to learn about construction codes and permits. It is always a good idea to work with a professional designer or architect to create a detailed construction plan.

After

Before

A patio enclosure offers the benefits of a permanent structure, but it can be built with inexpensive outdoor building materials using only basic rough carpentry skills.

Anatomy of a Patio Enclosure

Most patio enclosure structures have three basic elements: the foundation and the floor; the walls, windows, and doors; and the roof system. Of these, the roof system is the most challenging element for the do-it-yourselfer. There are a variety of patio roof products to choose from, but one of the most economical solutions is to install a corrugated roof panel system. Corrugated panel systems are installed over a network of rafters and spacers, called "purlins." The rafters can be tricky to install because they must be trimmed at an angle where they meet the house. If the cutting angle for the rafters is not indicated on your construction plan, consult an engineer or a building construction reference book to find the required angle.

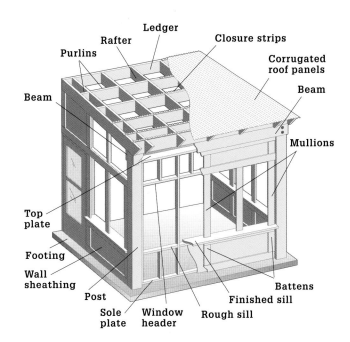

Planning a Patio Enclosure Project

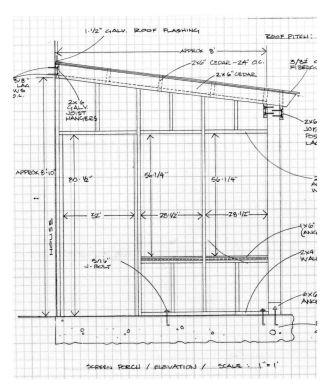

Work from a blueprint or plan. Consult a professional architect or designer to help you design a project that meets your needs. Working from approved plans that are created with professional input is a key factor in the success of any patio enclosure project.

Create footings for the patio enclosure walls. Check with your building department for code requirements. One way to create a footing for walls is to dig a trench around the concrete slab, to the required width and depth. Pour concrete into the trench using building paper or fiberboard to form an isolation joint that keeps the footing from bonding to the old concrete. If you do not have experience working with concrete, get additional information before you start.

How to Install Footings, Posts & Roofs

Tools & Materials ▸

Basic hand tools
Speed square
Caulk gun
Construction plan
Concrete
J-bolts
Post anchors
Wood posts (6 × 6")
Framing lumber
Joist hangers
Roof materials
　(photo, right)
Flashing
Lag screws
Deck screws
Nails
Caulk
Circular saw
Reciprocating saw
Washers and nuts
　for J-bolts

Drip-edge flashing
Self-tapping
　masonry screws
　(for stucco)
Stop molding
Storm door
Combination
　storm windows
1 × 4 cedar
Miter box
Exterior siding
Trim boards
Siding nails

Tip ▸

Corrugated roof systems are inexpensive and easy to construct with corrugated roof panels made of fiberglass or PVC. Sold in a variety of colors and transparencies, fiberglass panels are more rigid and let in more light than PVC panels. PVC panels are available in a wide selection of colors. Roofing panels are also available in different lengths, so you can cover the roof without creating horizontal seams. All corrugated roofing panels require closure strips that attach to the rafters to close off the space below the peaks in the panels. Use wood closure strips for fiberglass panels and foam closure strips for PVC panels.

1

*J-bolt locations for project as shown

Planned door location

J-bolt

Create a frost footing for the patio enclosure walls around the perimeter of the patio. Before the concrete for the footing dries, use the post locations from your plan as a reference for setting J-bolts into the concrete (inset). Install a J-bolt at the centerpoint for each planned post and at 3-ft. intervals in the area where the sole plates will be attached. Do not set J-bolts at the door location. Let the footing cure for at least three days before installing post anchors.

2

Ledger board
cutout area

Mark a cutout area to remove siding for the ledger board that will support the rafters and anchor the patio enclosure to your house. Measure up from the patio at both ends of the project area, and mark the height of the patio enclosure, including the thickness of the roof, onto the wall at each end. Add ½" for roof flashing (step 3 photo), then snap a chalk line between the points to mark the top of the cutout area. Add the width of the ledger board, the thickness of the roof, and ½". Measure down that amount from the chalk line, mark points, and snap a chalk line for the bottom of the cutout area. Mark the ends of the cutout area even with the outside faces of the posts in their planned locations.

3

½" for flashing
Thickness of roof
Width of ledger board
Top of cutout area

Remove the siding in the cutout area using a circular saw. Attach a 2 × 6 ledger board in the cutout area with 3½" lag screws driven at stud locations. The bottom of the board should be flush with the bottom of the cutout.

4

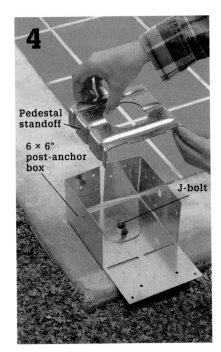

Pedestal standoff
6 × 6" post-anchor box
J-bolt

Secure post anchors to J-bolts with washers and nuts. *Note: Post anchors for 6 × 6" posts have a pedestal insert that fits into the anchor box. Cut and install the posts.*

5

Ledger board
Level line
Chalk/cutting line
Roof slope line

Once the ledger and the posts are set, use the slope of the planned roof to mark the tops of the posts for trimming. If your planned roof has a slope of 1½" per foot (as shown above), measure down from the level line on the posts 1½" for every foot of distance between the ledger and the posts. Mark a sloped cutting line across the face of the posts, then cut off the posts along this line with a handsaw.

(continued)

6

Guide

7

Install the beams. First, cut two 2 × 6 beams the same length as the ledger. Tack a strip of wood to the top of each post as a guide. With a helper, tack a beam to the front of one post with duplex nails, so the ends are flush with the outside face of the post, and the top is pressed up to the guide. Tack the other end. Attach another beam to the backs of the posts, pressed up to the guides. Drill counterbored pilot holes for ½ × 4"-long lag screws, then screw each beam to the posts with two lag screws at each end.

Mark and cut the rafters from 2 × 6s, ganged together for marking and cutting. Use a speed square to mark the cutting angles for the ends of the rafters where they meet the ledger (see construction plan). Draw a cutting line at the front end of the rafter so the rafter overhangs the front beam by at least ½" (for decorative appeal, angle-cut the front end to match the ledger end). Mark locations for "purlins" between rafters (step 9) on the edges of the rafters, spaced 24" on center.

8

Mark the rafter locations onto the ledger and the tops of the beams, following your construction plans (24" on center is standard). *Note: To provide a framework for the patio enclosure walls, we installed rafters on both sides of the posts. (Install joist hangers with joist-hanger nails at the rafter locations on the ledger. Set the rafters on the beams with the other ends in the joist hangers. Attach rafters to the joist hangers with joist-hanger nails. Toenail the front rafter ends to the beam with 8d nails at layout lines.)* Option: You may use rafter ties to attach the rafters to the beams.

9

Purlins

Planned wall location

Purlins are spacers that fit between the rafters, flush with the tops, to create a nailing surface for the strips used to mount most panel roof systems. Cut purlins from the same dimension lumber as the rafters, and nail them between the rafters with 8d nails (endnailing through the rafters where possible, toenailing in tighter spots). Use the layout lines drawn on the rafters in step 7 as an installation guide. *Note: In our plan, we used 2 × 4s for purlins that fit over the planned wall locations, to allow clearance for the top plate that fits between the outer rafters.*

10

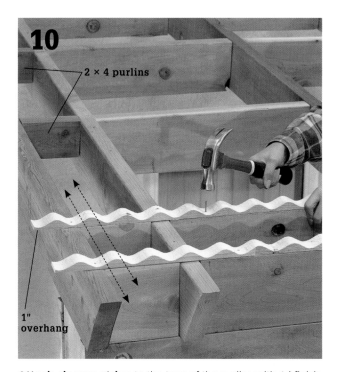

2 × 4 purlins

1" overhang

Attach closure strips to the tops of the purlins with 6d finish nails. The strips should overhang the outer rafters by 1". Proper alignment of the roof panels depends on the alignment of the closure strips, so attach the strips from the same end for proper alignment.

11

Measure from the back of the ledger cutout to the ends of the rafters, add 1" for a roof overhang, and cut roof panels to that length using a circular saw with a panel-cutting blade. For easier cutting, gang panels together, sandwiching them between two boards.

(continued)

12

Overlap
(rafter location)

Begin installing the roof panels. Panels are manufactured so the seams will line up over rafters that are spaced 24" on center. You may need to ripcut the first panel to span two rafters that are less than 24" apart, as in the photo above. Make sure the panels fit snugly over the closure strips mounted to the purlins. Attach the panels through the peaks, not the troughs, at each purlin location, by driving a 1½" hex-head panel screw with a rubber gasket at every fourth or fifth peak. Predrill through the panel at each screw location using a bit that is slightly larger than the diameter of the screw shank. Apply caulk in the trough nearest the panel seam before attaching the next panel (see step 14).

13

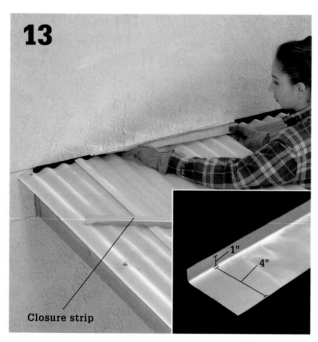

1"
4"

Closure strip

After installing one or two panels, begin installing flashing between the roof and the wall. Cut strips of 5"-wide galvanized roll flashing and bend them to create a 1" flange using a 2 × 4 as a bending jig (inset). Tuck the 1"-wide flange behind the wall covering, then apply caulk to the flat face of a piece of the closure strip and insert it between the panels and the underside of the flashing.

14

Continue installing the roof panels and flashing, making sure that the panel seams line up over the rafters and that the strips of flashing overlap by 3 to 4". Remember to apply caulk to the last trough of each panel so it creates a waterproof seam with the first peak of the next panel.

How to Install Walls, Windows & Doors

1

Cut 2 × 4 sole plates from pressure-treated lumber, sized to fit against the posts and the house wall on all three exposed sides of the patio. Set the sole plates next to the J-bolts installed in the footing, and mark the locations of the J-bolts onto the plates with a square. Drill centered guide holes into the sole plates at the J-bolt locations.

2

Set the sole plates over the footings so the guide holes slip over the J-bolts. Secure the sole plates by attaching washers and nuts to the J-bolts.

3

Mark locations for the wall framing members onto the sole plates using your construction plan as a guide. Mark the opening for the door and the jambs onto the sole plate—usually ⅜" wider than the width of the door.

4

Cut 2 × 4s for full-height framing members so they are 2" longer than their finished height. Set them in position onto the sole plates, and use a level to adjust each 2 × 4 until it is plumb. Mark cutting lines on the 2 × 4 where it meets the bottom of the outer rafter. Also mark the position of the 2 × 4 onto the rafters. Cut at cutting lines.

(continued)

Cut and install the top plates. For this project, we installed 2 × 6 plates between the outer rafters and beams—5½"-wide spaces based on the width of the posts. Cut two top plates to span the distance between the ledger and the beam at the front of the patio enclosure. Cut a plate to fit in front, between the two posts. Nail the top plates in place flush with the bottom of the rafters or beams. Here, we nailed through the rafters into the sides of the plates with 10d nails on the sides of the patio enclosure, and we nailed through the beams in front.

Toenail full-height framing members to the top plates at the locations marked on the rafter and to the sole plates at layout marks. Use 10d nails. Check with a level to make sure framing members are plumb.

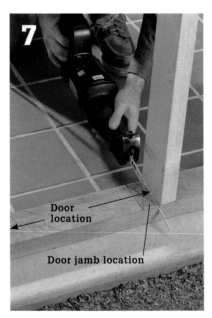

Cut and remove the sole plate at the door location using a reciprocating saw. Make sure you cut next to the framing member marks on your layout. The door jambs should rest on the floor, not the sole plate.

Install the door jambs. For this project, we used 2 × 6 lumber for the jambs, creating a frame for the door that is centered on the 2 × 4 framing members. Because our door is located next to the house, we attached the inside jamb directly to the siding using self-tapping masonry screws.

Install the door header on top of the door jambs. Our jambs were cut to the rough opening height for the door, so we simply endnailed the 2 × 6 header into the tops of the jambs with 10d nails.

10

Install the 2 × 4 headers for the window rough openings, according to your construction plan (window headers usually are installed at the same height as door headers). To set the height for the window headers, attach one end of a chalk line to the top of the door header, slip a line level onto the chalk line, set the line at a level position, and snap it across the other framing members.

11

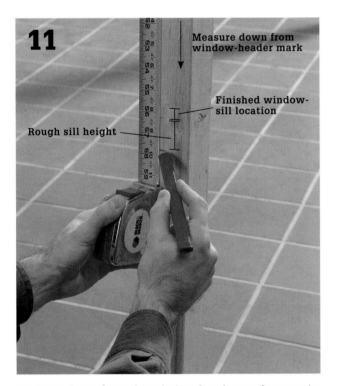

Measure down from window-header mark

Finished window-sill location

Rough sill height

Measure down from the window header marks to mark positions for the rough windowsills onto the framing members and posts. Remember to include the thickness of the finished windowsill in the rough opening measurement (see step 14 and your construction plan).

12

Cut the window headers and the rough sills to length from 2 × 4 stock. Install them between the framing members by endnailing through the framing members and into the headers and rough sills where possible. Otherwise, toenail the headers and rough sills in place.

(continued)

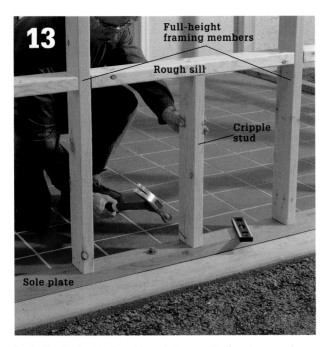

Install cripple studs midway between the framing members, fitted between the rough sills and the sole plates, and between the headers and the top plates. Where they meet the top plates, cut the tops of the cripple studs to match the angle of the cuts on the full-height framing members.

Install finished windowsills with a slight slope to direct water runoff away from the structure. To create the slope, tack ¼"-thick sill spacers to the tops of the rough sills, flush with the inside edges. Then, cut the finished sills and attach them to the rough sills with 10d nails so they extend 1" past the edges of the rough sills.

Combination storm windows are attached to strips of window-stop molding (we used 1 × 2 pine) mounted at the top and sides of the window opening. Cut strips of 1 × 2 the same length as the headers, then nail them to the bottoms of the headers, flush with the inside edges. Then, cut strips to span from the finished sill to the header strips, and attach them to the jambs with 6d casing nails.

Apply a bead of caulk to the outside edges of the 1 × 2 window-stop strips. Set each window in position in the rough opening, pressing it into the caulk beads. Leave a slight gap for drainage between the bottom of the window and the finished sill. *Note: Combination storm windows usually are not fastened at the bottom.*

17

Make sure the window is level and square in the rough opening, then drill pilot holes for #4 × 1" hex-head sheet-metal screws into the flanges of the window. Attach the window starting at the top corners, driving three fasteners into each flange. Install all of the windows.

18

1 × 4 mullion strip

Cover the exposed framing members with 1 × 4 lumber (we used cedar) cut to fit between the window headers and the finished sills. Install the 1 × 4s, called "mullions," so they are centered on the framing members. Use 8d siding nails.

19

Install a combination storm door in the door's rough opening, following the manufacturer's directions.

How to Install Wall Coverings & Trim

To create the exterior walls of our patio enclosure, we used ¼"-thick rough cedar siding panels and 1 × 4 cedar boards to cover the edges and seams (called "battens"). Start with the wall areas below the windows, cutting siding panels to fit the space between the windowsill and the ground—leave a ¼" gap at the bottom. Cut siding panels so the seams fall over framing members, leaving a ⅛" to ¼"-wide expansion gap between panels. Attach the panels to the framing members with 4d galvanized siding nails.

Install trim strips (we used 1 × 4 cedar batten boards) to trim the seams at the tops and bottoms of the siding panels and to cover the joints between the panels. Arrange the strips so the tops and bottoms run the full length of the wall, if possible, and fill in vertical strips to make butt joints at the tops and bottoms. Use 4d siding nails to attach the batten boards.

Before installing the siding above the windows and doors, cut strips of drip-edge flashing and attach them to the headers with caulk—do not use fasteners. Drip-edge flashing directs water away from the framing members.

4

Install siding panels between the headers and the top plates. Cut the siding pieces for the side walls so the top angle matches the slope of the roof line. Attach siding panels, then cut and install battens for the tops and bottoms, and to cover vertical joints. *Note: You may need to rip-cut the bottom batten to fit around the door header, depending on the construction method used.*

5

Caulk all exposed seams, using exterior caulk that is tinted to match the color of the siding.

6

Install 1 × 4 cedar mullions on the inside faces of the vertical framing members, then cut and install siding panels on the interior sides of the walls using the same techniques used on the exterior. For the interior of our project, we used the same ¼"-thick cedar siding used on the exterior. Instead of 1 × 4 cedar battens, we used pine ranch moldings at the bases of the panels, which were cut to full wall length so there were no seams to cover.

7

Install the remaining interior trim. We used ranch-style baseboards, mitered at the corners. We also installed pine quarter-round molding at the corner joints. If you are using cedar for the trim, no further finishing is required. If you are using pine or exterior-grade plywood, seal or paint the wood for protection and to improve the appearance.

Patio Arbor/Trellis Enclosure

An arbor is an overhead system of beams, usually supported by posts, that provides shade and is often used to train climbing plants. Arbors can be built as independent yard structures, but they often are combined with a trellis—a lattice wall attached to the side of the arbor (pages 154 to 155). The combined arbor-and-trellis is a traditional, attractive outdoor structure.

Build your arbor structure so it is freestanding—do not attach it directly to your house. A permanent structure that is attached to a house must meet more code requirements than freestanding structures, and there is more risk of structural failure. The arbor featured in this section is made with four-post construction set on sturdy concrete footings. Because it is freestanding, the footings did not need to extend below the frost line. Very small garden arbors can be built with techniques and materials similar to those used for the project shown, but they may not require post footings.

Arbor structures make a dramatic visual statement when constructed over an ordinary patio. They also help cut down on wind and sun and create a more pleasant outdoor environment.

Freestanding Arbors ▸

An arbor does not need to be attached to your house to function as a patio shelter. In fact, more arbors are built as freestanding units than as attached structures. Because they are so versatile you can locate them so they cast shade only on a portion of a patio, or you can cover the entire area.

The arbor shown here is relatively small. You can easily adapt the design to different sizes, but don't space the posts more than 8 ft. apart. If you want to build a larger arbor, add additional posts between the corner posts. Before you begin construction, check your local building code for footing depth requirements and setback restrictions.

The basics of building a freestanding arbor are as follows. First, lay out the location of the posts using stakes and string. Make sure the layout is square by measuring from corner to corner and adjusting the layout until these diagonal measurements are equal. Dig postholes at the corners to the required depth, using a posthole digger and fill each hole with 6" of gravel.

Next, position the posts in the holes. To brace them in a plumb position, tack support boards to the posts on adjoining faces. Adjust the posts as necessary until they're plumb. Drive a stake into the ground, flush against the base of each 2 × 4. Drive deck screws through the stakes, into the 2 × 4s.

Mix one bag of dry concrete to anchor each post. Immediately check to make sure the posts are plumb, and adjust as necessary until the concrete begins to harden. Let the concrete dry at least 24 hours.

Measure, mark, and cut all the lumber for the arbor. Cut a 3 × 3" notch off the bottom corner of each tie beam, a 2 × 2" notch off the bottom corner of each 2 × 4 rafter, and a 1 × 1" notch off the bottom corner of each cross strip. Position a tie beam against the outside edge of a pair of posts, 7 ft. above the ground. Position the beam to extend about 1 ft. past the post on each side. Level the beam, then clamp it into place with wood screw clamps. Drill pilot holes and attach the tie beam to the posts with 3" lag screws.

Use a line level to mark the opposite pair of posts at the same height as the installed tie beam. Attach the remaining tie beam. Cut off the posts so they're level with the tops of the tie beams.

Next, attach the rafters to the tops of the tie beams, using rafter ties and galvanized nails. Beginning 6" from the ends of the tie beams, space the rafters

2 ft. apart, with the ends extending past each tie beam by 1 ft. Position a cross strip across the top of the rafters, beginning 6" from the ends of the rafters. Center the strip so it extends past the outside rafters by about 6". Drill pilot holes through the cross strip and into the rafters. Attach the cross strip with galvanized screws. Add the remaining cross strips, spacing them 1 ft. apart. Finish your arbor by applying wood sealer/protectant.

This version of a freestanding post-and-slat arbor is a 5 × 5-ft. cedar structure with an extended overhead.

How to Build Arbors

Create footings for the arbor posts by digging a hole at least twice the size of the post bottom and at least 12" deep. Fill with concrete, and set a J-bolt in each concrete footing. We positioned the J-bolts so the edges of the posts are flush with the patio.

Allow the footings to harden for at least one day, then attach the post anchor hardware to the J-bolts. Cut and install the arbor posts—for most arbors, 4 × 4 posts are large enough. Cut posts longer than the planned height, and brace them with 2 × 4 braces so they are plumb. Leave the braces in place until the beams and rafters are secured in position.

Use a square to mark the cutting lines for the posts at the desired height: mark the height of the arbor onto the posts at one end, then use a line level to transfer the height mark onto the posts at the other end. With a square, mark cutting lines on all four sides of each post. Trim the posts at the cutting lines using a handsaw. Have a helper steady the post from below while you cut. *Note: You may use a power saw, like a cordless circular saw, to cut off the post tops, but only if your ladder provides enough elevation that you can work from above the cutting line.*

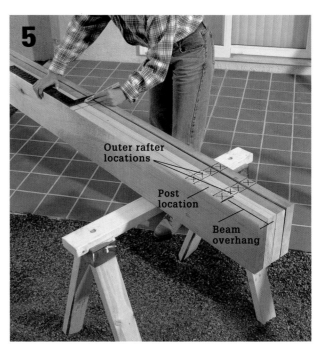

Cut beam members from 2 × 8 stock. Because we used two beam members each at the front and back of the project, we cut four beam members. To create a 6" overhang at each side, we cut the beam members 12" longer than the distance between the outside edges of the posts. Mark all beam members with a carpenter's square, then gang-cut them with a circular saw and a straightedge.

Turn beams on edge, and mark locations for the rafters. Rafters should be no more than 24" apart. Start by marking the outermost rafters—our plan called for a rafter at the inside and outside edge of each post. Don't forget to include the beam overhang in the layout.

Fasten the beam members to the posts at the front and back of the arbor. Screw a guide strip securely to the top of each post, then position the beam members and hold them in place temporarily by driving a screw down through the guide strip and into the top of each beam member. When installing beam pairs, as shown here, use a pair of carriage bolts with washers and nuts at each beam/post joint. Attach a ½" bit with a bit extension to your drill, and drill holes for the carriage bolts through both the beam members and the post.

(continued)

7

Pound ½"-diameter carriage bolts through the holes. Carriage bolts should be ½" to 1" longer than the combined widths of the outer rafters and the beam. For this project, we used a 7"-long bolt. Slip a washer and nut onto the end of the carriage bolt and tighten with a ratchet. Remove the guide strip.

8

Measure and mark 2 × 6 rafters to fit on top of the beams, perpendicular to the house. For best appearance, rafters should overhang the beams by at least 6". Cut with a circular saw. For added visual appeal, mark an angled cut of about 30° at the end of one rafter, then cut off with a circular saw. Use the rafter as a template to transfer the angle to the other rafters.

9

Rafter tie

Install the rafters on top of the beams at the rafter layout marks. Position the rafters so the angled ends are at the front of the project, with the shorter side resting on the beam. Use metal rafter ties, mounted to the beams, and deck screws to attach the rafters. *Option: Because the metal rafter ties can be quite visible in the finished product, you may prefer to toenail the rafters in place with 16d galvanized nails.*

10

Beam mark

Crossbrace location

Post mark

18"

18"

Mark the posts and beams for crossbraces. From the inside corner of each post/beam joint, mark an equal distance (about 18") on the beam and the post. For crossbraces that fit between rafters, measure from the post mark to the top of the rafter, following the line created between the post mark and the beam mark. For crossbraces that fit flush with the post and the beam, measure from the post mark to the beam mark for the inside dimension of the crossbrace.

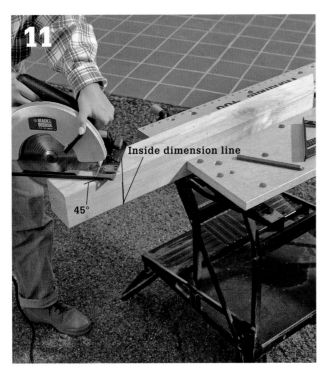

11

Inside dimension line

45°

Mark the inside dimensions for the crossbraces onto a piece of lumber of the same type as the posts (here, 4 × 4). Use a square or triangle to draw 45° cutting lines away from each end point of the inside dimension. Cut along these lines with a circular saw to make the crossbraces.

12

Install the crossbraces. Tack the crossbraces in position, then attach them with ⅜" × 4" lag screws. If the crossbrace is fitted between the rafters, drive the lag screws through the counterbored pilot holes in the rafter and into the cross brace at the top. Attach with lag screws at each joint. Drive lag screws through the counterbored pilot holes that are perpendicular to the post or rafter.

13

Install the arbor slats on top of the rafters. We used 2 × 2 cedar spaced at 4" intervals. Include an overhang of at least 6". Attach the arbor slats with 2½" deck screws driven down through the slats and into the rafters.

Adding a Trellis to an Arbor

Add a lattice-panel trellis to an arbor structure for a more decorative appearance. Using manufactured lattice panels and lattice molding and hanging the panels with metal fence-panel hangers makes the job inexpensive and quick. Or, you can build your own lattice and frame. Plant climbing-type plants and train them up the trellis to embellish the arbor-and-trellis.

Tools & Materials ▶

Pencil
Tape measure
Circular saw
Chalk line
Hammer

Drill
4 × 8 lattice panels
Lattice molding
Galvanized brads
Fence brackets

Lattice panels are used to create the trellis portion of an arbor-and-trellis. Most building centers carry cedar, pressure-treated, and vinyl lattice in 2-ft. × 8-ft. and 4-ft. × 8-ft. panels. Standard lattice panels are ¾" thick. For a more customized look, you can build your own lattice panels from exterior-rated lumber.

How to Add a Trellis to an Arbor

If the planned trellis is wider than 4 ft., you will need additional support posts. Install posts using the same materials and techniques used for the corner posts of the arbor. If possible, install the posts so the lattice panels on either side of each post will be equal in size.

Measure the openings between the posts to determine the sizes for the lattice panels. Generally, panels should be sized so they are installed below the crossbraces between posts. Leave a few inches of open space beneath the panels at ground level. Mark the locations of the panel tops onto the posts using a level to make sure the tops are even.

Subtract 1½" from the frame opening dimensions, and cut the lattice panels to size. To cut lattice panels, sandwich each panel between two boards near the cutting line to prevent the lattice from separating. Clamp the boards and the panel together and cut with a circular saw.

Miter-cut 2 × 2 lattice molding to frame the lattice panels. The finished width of the panel should be ½" narrower than the opening. Nail one vertical and one horizontal frame piece together with galvanized brads. Set the lattice panel into the channels, and attach the other frame pieces. Secure the lattice panels into the molding by driving brads through the molding and into the lattice at 12" intervals.

Attach three fence brackets to the posts, evenly spaced, on each side of the opening using 4d galvanized nails. On the top two brackets, bend the bottom and top flanges flat against the post. Bend all outside flanges flat, away from the post, to allow installation of the lattice panel.

Set the panels in the brackets, and bend the hanger flanges back to their original positions. Drive 1" galvanized nails through the flanges of the fence hangers and into the frames of the lattice panels.

Three-Season Porch

A three-season porch blends indoor comfort with an outdoor atmosphere. It is a transition space between your home and yard. Windows with self-storing screens line each wall to provide plenty of fresh air and an enjoyable view of your landscape, while keeping insects and inclement weather at bay.

Building a three-season porch is an ambitious project, but like any large-scale project, it can be divided into simple, manageable steps, making the construction process less daunting. Because each building situation is different, you'll need to create your own plans and plan drawings to reflect the specific details and dimensions of your home and yard. For example, the distance from the ground to your home's entrance will vary, affecting the height of the deck frame posts and the steps and landing. Make sure all plans comply with your local building codes and zoning laws. You will need to submit complete plan drawings, including an elevation drawing and a floor plan, along with an estimated cost of materials in order to be issued a building permit.

Tools & Materials ▶

Circular saw	Stapler	Joist-hanger nails	15# building paper
Drill/driver	Jigsaw	Box nails	Compactible gravel
Caulk gun	Hammer drill	Siding nails	12"-dia. concrete
Power auger	2 × 2s	Roofing nails	footing forms
or clamshell digger	2 × 4s	Finish nails	Concrete
Reciprocating saw	Lag screws	Deck screws	Flashing
Handsaw	J-bolts	Masonry screws	Asphalt shingles
Wheelbarrow	Joist hangers	2 × 4 trusses	Windows with
Shovel	Post anchors	(8-in-12 pitch)	self-storing screens
Hand tamper	Angle brackets	Siding	Combination storm
T-bevel	H-clips	Silicone caulk	door and threshold
Power miter saw	Hurricane ties	Construction adhesive	12 × 12" aluminum
Nailset	Common nails	Roofing cement	louvered vent

Three-season porches add living space to your home. Typically, they are wired with lights and electrical service, but they are not hooked into your heating and cooling system.

How to Build a Three-Season Porch

Attach the ledger. Measure and mark the center of your entrance, then measure out from that centerpoint in both directions and mark for the ends of the ledger outline. Draw an outline 2" below the door threshold to lay out the ledger position. Remove the siding within the outlined area and position the ledger in the cutout. Brace the ledger with 2 × 4s and tack it in place with 10d common nails. Fasten the ledger to the rim joist with counterbored ⅜ × 4" lag screws and washers. Cover the heads of the lag screws with silicone caulk.

Locate the footings. Build and set up batterboards that are aligned with the post locations. Run mason's strings from one set of batterboards to the ledger and between the other set of batterboards and level them using a line level. Make sure the strings are perpendicular and mark the centerpoints of the footings on the strings. Transfer the centerpoints of the footings to the ground, using a plumb bob. Mark each point with a stake.

Pour the footings. Remove the mason's strings and dig holes for 12"-dia. footings using a power auger or a clamshell digger. Pour 2 to 3" of compactible gravel into each hole for drainage. Cut 12"-dia. concrete tube forms to length and set them into the footing holes so the tops are level and 2" above ground. Make sure the tops of the forms are level, then pack soil around them for support. Mix concrete and fill each form. Set 6" J-bolts in the centers of the footings before the concrete sets. Let the concrete cure for two to three days.

Set the posts. Fasten a 6 × 6 metal post anchor on each footing, centered over the J-bolt. Cut 6 × 6 posts at least 6" longer than the required post height and set the posts in the anchors. Tack each post with a nail and brace with 1 × 4s and stakes. Run a level mason's line from the bottom of the ledger to one end post, and run another level string across all the posts at the bottom of ledger height. Mark cutting lines at the string height and then move and cut the posts to length. Replace the posts, check for plumb, and fasten with 16d galvanized nails.

(continued)

Build the floor frame. Cut the doubled rim joist boards to length and bind them together with construction adhesive and 10d nails. Lay out matching joist hanger locations on the ledger and the inside face of the rim joist. Attach joist hangers with 10d galvanized nails. Then, position the rim joist on the posts and tack with nails. Cut the joists to length and make double joists for the ends and the middle, leaving the inner board of each doubled end joist 1½" shorter than the outer board at the ledger end only. Install the end joists by facenailing to the end of the ledger at the house and nailing through the rim joist and into the joist ends at the posts. Check for square and reinforce the corners at the posts with metal corner braces. Cut and hang the joists, fastening with 10d joist-hanger nails.

Install the joist blocking. From the ledger, measure along the top of both end joists and mark a reference at the midpoint. Connect the reference lines with a chalk line between the marks and then measure and cut 2 × 10 blocking to fit in each bay between the joists. End nail the blocks to the joists with 16d galvanized common nails, staggering the pattern along the chalk line.

Remove the siding. Outline the porch walls (but not the roof) onto the house siding. Set your circular saw blade to the depth equal to the thickness of the house siding, and cut along the outline. Finish the cuts in the corners with a handsaw. Remove the siding pieces using a pry bar.

Option: If the end studs of the porch walls will not be located at a house wall stud location, install 2 × 4 blocking in the stud bay where the porch walls tie in. In each stud bay that will contain blocking, mark for blocking against the bottom plate, then measure up and mark the studs every 24" up to the top plate. Also mark for blocking at the top plate. Cut 2 × 4s to size and install them in pairs using 16d common nails.

Install the subfloor. Beginning next to the house, install a full sheet of ⅝ or ¾" exterior-grade, tongue-and-groove subflooring. Apply a bead of construction adhesive to the joist tops first, and nail the subfloor with 8d box nails spaced every 6" along the edges and 12" in the field. (You can use 2½" deck screws instead.) If necessary, trim the sheet so the edges fall on the center of a joist. Cut the next piece to size and install, leaving a ⅛" gap. Install the next row, beginning with a half sheet so the joints are staggered.

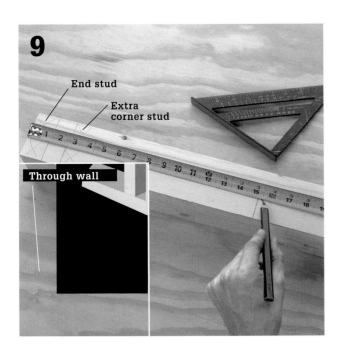

Lay out wall frames. Use a pencil and a speed square to begin marking the wall stud locations on the sole plates and the cap plates for the porch walls. Include marks for extra corner studs in walls that will butt up against another wall (inset).

Build headers. Construct headers by sandwiching together pairs of 2× lumber with a piece of ½" plywood in the middle. This will create strong beams that are the same thickness as dimensional lumber (3½"). Use construction adhesive and 10d common nails to fasten the beam members together.

(continued)

Frame the walls. Assemble the walls one at a time using 16d common nails for endnailing and 10d common nails for toenailing. Use 8d box nails to fasten the 2 × 4 blocking between the king studs and the common studs at the ends of the walls. Raise the walls one at a time and brace them with 2 × 4s staked to the ground. Begin with the side wall, followed by the door wall, and finally the end wall. Make sure each wall is plumb, then fasten it to the floor frame with 16d common nails spaced every 16", but do not nail through the bottom plate in the door's rough opening. Tie the walls together and to the house with 16d common nails.

Install the first truss. Locate the framing members of the house and draw reference lines on the outside wall up to the planned roof peak. With help, hoist the first truss into position against the house. Align the peak of the truss with the centerline marked on the siding. The truss should be flush against the siding and the rafter tails should overhang the top plates equally. Nail the chords of the truss to the framing members of the house using 20d common nails.

Install the remaining trusses. Lay out the remaining truss locations every 16" on-center on the top plates of both the side wall and the door wall. Lift the remaining trusses into place and install them, working away from the house. Make sure the rafter tails overhang the top plates equally. Toenail through the bottom chords with 10d common nails to fasten. Reinforce the trusses with hurricane ties (inset) attached by driving 8d common nails into the top plate and 8d joist-hanger nails into the rafter chords.

Build the gable wall. On the top plate of the end wall, mark the gable wall stud locations every 16" on center. Set the two 2 × 4 gable plates on edge and use a speed square (inset photo) to mark the pitch for the peak at one end. Cut the peak ends and fasten with 10d common nails. Transfer the stud layout marks from the end wall to the gable plates. Cut the gable wall studs to length, trimming the top ends to match the roof pitch. Toenail the studs to the end wall and endnail through the gable plates using 10d common nails.

Build the gable overhang. From the peak of the gable-end truss, measure down along each rafter chord and mark the lookout layout. Use a speed square to transfer the marks to the faces of the rafter chords. Transfer the lookout locations to the top of the gable plates. Cut 2 × 4 lookouts and align them with the location lines. Fasten them to the rafter chords and gable plates with 10d common nails. At the peak, fasten a lookout so it's plumb and the corners are flush with the top edges of the rafter chords. Cut barge rafters to fit and attach them to the ends of the lookouts.

Install the roof sheathing. Cut ½" exterior-grade plywood or oriented-strand board sheathing to cover the trusses and the gable overhang. Install sheathing from the rafter tails to the peak, using 8d box nails driven every 6" along the edges and 12" in the field of the sheets. The sheathing should not protrude beyond the rafter tail ends, and any seams should fall on rafter chords. Use metal H-clips (inset) between sheets to ensure a ⅛" gap at horizontal seams, and leave a ¼" gap at the peak.

Attach the fascia. Use a speed square to mark one end of the two 1 × 6 gable fascia boards to match the roof pitch. Cut the peak ends, then measure and cut each board long enough to extend several inches past the ends of the rafter tails. Position the fascia boards so the top edges are flush with the sheathing. Fasten the fascia with 8d galvanized finish nails. Cut side fascia boards to length and install so the tops of the boards do not project above the sheathing. Trim the ends of the gable fascia boards so they are flush with the side fascia boards.

(continued)

Install the roof covering. Cut away the house siding about 2" above the roof sheathing. Install drip edge flashing at the eaves and then staple overlapping courses of 15# building paper to the roof deck, starting at the eaves. Install drip edge along the gable ends then shingle and complete the flashing. If you have not installed roof coverings before, refer to a roofing book for more information.

Attach the wall sheathing and housewrap. Attach ½" exterior-grade plywood sheathing to the porch framing, using 2" deck screws or 6d box nails driven every 6" along the edges and every 12" in the field area. Make sure all seams fall on studs. Apply house wrap or 15# building paper in horizontal strips over all of the wall surfaces using staples spaced roughly 12" apart. Also wrap the framed door and window openings with building paper or self-adhesive window flashing.

Window sill   Sill nailer

Attach the window sills. Cut 1 × 2 sill nailers for the end wall, side wall, and door wall. Align each nailer flush with the interior edge of the rough sills and fasten it with 4d box nails. Cut 2 × 8 window sills and install them in the rough openings so they slope downward and their back edges extend out 1" past the interior edges of the rough openings. Fasten the sills with 16d galvanized finish nails.

Install the windows. At each window rough opening, install nailers 1" from the inside edges of the framed openings to create installation surfaces for the windows. Use 2 × 2 for the horizontal nailers and 1 × 2 for the vertical nailers. Place the combination storm windows against the nailers so the flanges are roughly ¾" from the framing members of the walls. Make sure all windows are plumb, then fasten them to the nailers using the screws specified by the window manufacturer. Run a thick caulk bead between the windows and the sills.

Frame the door opening. Measure, mark, and cut finish-grade 1 × 6 lumber to size for the door jambs. Rip the pieces to width, if necessary. Install the jambs for the door header and the latch flush with the sheathing using 8d casing nails. For the hinge-side jamb, align flush with sheathing and shim as necessary so that the door opening is ⅛" to ¼" wider than the door itself.

Install the door. *Note: Read and follow the manufacturer's instructions for your storm door before installation. Position the door in the framed opening so the hinge side of the door is tight against the door jamb. Drill guide holes spaced every 12" through the hinge-side frame and into the sheathing. Attach the frame with mounting screws (provided with door). With the door closed, drill guide holes and attach the latch-side frame to the sheathing. Keep an even gap between the door and the frame. Center the door frame top piece on top of the frame sides. Drill pilot holes and fasten it to the door header. Attach lock and latch hardware as directed.*

Install the soffit panels. Cut soffit panels to size from ¼" exterior-grade plywood. Install the panels at the gable-end overhang first, then along the side wall and door wall eaves. Hold each panel flush against the lookouts or rafter tails, with the front edge tight against the fascia boards, and fasten using 4d galvanized casing nails.

(continued)

25 Door header trim — Header trim — Inner window trim — End trim — Sill trim

Install the trim. Measure and cut the inner window trim for each window from 1 × 2 cedar, beginning with the horizontal pieces at the header. Install them flush with the exterior face of the wall sheathing, with the back edges against the window flanges using 4d galvanized finish nails. Cut the corner trim pieces so they extend from 1" below the bottom edge of the wall sheathing up to the soffits. Rip the boards to width if necessary and notch them to fit around the window sills. Fasten them with 8d galvanized finish nails. Cut the end trim to fit from 1" below the bottom edge of the deck frame up to the soffits. Fasten with 8d galvanized finish nails. Cut the horizontal trim pieces (the header trim, sill trim, and skirt trim) and nail in place. Cut and install the vertical window trim. Finally, install the aluminum door threshold.

Install the gable vent. At the gable wall, mark the location for the vent, then drill ⅜" holes at each corner. Draw reference lines between the holes and cut at the lines using a jigsaw. Position the vent cover over the opening, making sure it is level, then fasten it to the sheathing with 4d galvanized box nails.

Install the siding. Cut 1"-wide strips from the top edge of the siding pieces to use as starter strips and install along the top edge of the base trim using siding nails. Cut the first course of siding to fit between the corner trim boards with a slight gap (⅛" or so). Attach with 6d siding nails driven at stud locations, about 1¼" down from the top edge. Install the next course so the bottom covers the siding nails on the course below. Finish the installation, maintaining a consistent reveal. Ripcut the final pieces to size, if necessary, and caulk all gaps and seams.

28

Landing wall

Facing boards

Top gusset

Step nailer

Bottom gusset

Add steps. Install steps to gain access to the porch. There are many types of steps you can build. Because the porch is attached to your house, any attached steps must be supported by footings that extend past the frostline. The concrete pad seen here is supported by such footings. The undercarriage for the steps, made from pressure-treated lumber, is essentially a mini-deck supported by a ledger on one end and a framed wall on the other end. The landing area must be at least 4 ft. wide and 3 ft. deep. The steps themselves are made with wood stringers that support wood risers and treads. In most areas, if you have more than two steps you are required to include a grippable handrail.

Interior Finishing Ideas ▶

Because a three-season porch is treated as an outdoor space, finish the interior using materials suited for indoor/ outdoor applications. They will hold up best over time and against exposure to the elements. Wood paneling or tongue-and-groove wainscoting (photo A) are the most practical choices for finishing the porch walls. Both are easy to install and are much more durable than wallboard.

Ceilings can also be finished with paneling or with a suspended ceiling system. Use finish-grade lumber or decorative moldings to trim out corners and windows (photo B). *Note: Before you finish the walls and ceiling, install all electrical receptacle and fixture boxes and run the cables from the main service panel. The porch should be wired on its own ground-fault protected (GFCI) circuit.*

A

B

Building Sunrooms

Like all porches and patio spaces, sunrooms help connect a home and its occupants with the outdoors. At the same time, sunrooms are meant to be enjoyed year-round in areas with four seasons. Therefore, the sunroom must function like a finished interior space. Building a sunroom isn't necessarily more difficult than building a porch or patio enclosure—in fact, with the many products and all-in-one packages available, the design and construction of a sunroom can be relatively simple—but planning for a new sunroom does require additional considerations, such as how to position the room for ideal sun exposure and how to keep the space comfortable in all seasons. This section begins with a complete discussion of special planning and design considerations for sunrooms, including a review of the usual options for getting the work done. In the projects that follow, you'll see three different real-life examples of how to create a sunroom from start to finish.

In this chapter:

- Planning a New Sunspace
- Sunporch
- Sunroom
- Hard-sided Greenhouse Kit

Planning a New Sunspace

A typical sunroom project can be a lot like putting on an addition. The new room expands, or bumps out from, the home's original footprint and includes all of the construction elements of an indoor space: a foundation and insulated floor, walls, and roof, plus electrical and heating and cooling systems for all your creature comforts. Also, like an addition, a sunroom can have a big impact on both the interior and exterior architecture of the home, and, if planned properly, it improves the quality and function of nearby rooms.

Because a sunroom is all about enjoying the light and warmth from the sun, deciding where to place the room is a critical consideration. Your choices of location may be limited by several factors, including the local zoning laws, so it's best to consult your city office at the beginning of the planning process. Another big decision lies in how the sunroom will be built. Most people prefer to hire out the project and either have a manufactured sunroom installed by a professional crew or go the custom route and have the room designed and built from scratch. But if you're handy and up to the job, you might choose to build a sunroom yourself using a complete kit.

It's also possible to create a sunroom without adding on. Given the right location and good sun exposure, an existing room can be turned into a sunroom by installing lots of windows and perhaps a new entry door. And some homeowners find they can save space and money (or satisfy zoning restrictions) by converting a roofed porch or patio or even an elevated deck into a sunroom.

Whatever your dreams for a sun-filled haven, this section introduces you to many of the basic considerations that go into planning and creating a sunroom. As you begin your research, consult with local building professionals and other expert sources for more advice that's specific to your project. Product manufacturers, companies that specialize in sunroom design and construction, and even neighbors who have sunrooms also can be valuable sources for information.

As year-round living space, a sunroom must be designed and built with accommodations for seasonal heating and/or cooling, air circulation, energy efficiency, security, and, of course, plenty of daylight.

Building Codes & Permits

No matter how you design it, a sunroom is living space. As such, it will most likely fall within the jurisdiction of your city's building code and zoning laws. This means your project will probably require a building permit, which includes passing various inspections during the construction phase. No big deal. Just call the building department and find out what the first step is. If you're working with a professional designer or builder, they may take care of most, or all, dealings with the building department for you.

Building codes and zoning laws are distinct aspects of local governance, but for anyone remodeling or, especially, adding onto a home, there are equally important legal matters to address. The building code establishes design and construction standards for all types of residential and commercial buildings in a given area. The code is enforced locally, typically through a city office or building department, and it takes into account local weather conditions, natural hazards (like termites), and other factors that can affect the health, safety, and longevity of structures.

Most building departments will not issue a permit for a project without first reviewing and approving a set of drawn plans. Some departments accept plans drawn by homeowners (but may require an architect's or engineer's stamp), while others require plans drafted by a professional, such as a licensed contractor, designer, or architect. If you are building your own sunroom or are acting as general contractor for the project, find out everything the building department requires for a building permit. For example, most require an accurate and realistic estimate of the materials costs, as the permit fee generally is calculated as a percentage of the cost. Local contractors who specialize in sunrooms should be very familiar with the permit process.

Zoning laws govern the use of, and alterations made to, private property. For a homeowner adding on a sunroom, several zoning restrictions may come into play. The most common rule that applies is setback. This is the minimum distance any part of a house must be from its property lines. Some cities let you build within inches of your lot boundaries; others require a setback of several feet or more. Zoning laws may also dictate how much of a lot can be developed. If your house takes up all the allotted space for your lot size, adding on might not be an option. Multistory or upper-level sunrooms may run up against height restrictions that limit their design.

If your plans run afoul of the local zoning laws, you may be allowed to apply for a variance with the zoning board. It is time to test your forensic skills and collect any relevant evidence to support your case. It pays to be prepared.

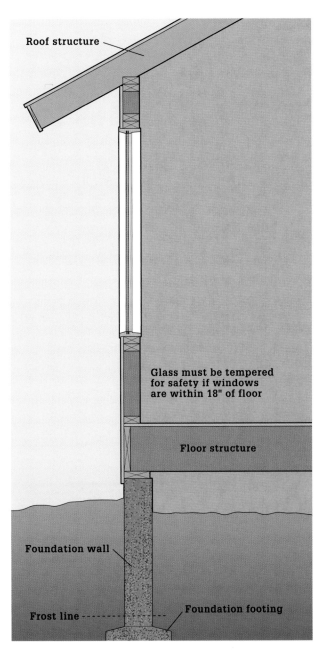

Research local building codes. When sunrooms are attached to a house, codes typically require a foundation that extends below the frost line (depth to which the ground freezes). Other common specifications include tempered glass on windows within 18" of the floor and roofs designed for snow loads, wind, and other local weather conditions.

Where to Put It

To answer the big question of where to locate your new sunroom, start by asking some more specific questions.

- What do you plan to do in the room?
- When will you use it most—at what time of day and in which seasons?
- How will the sunroom integrate with, and enhance, adjacent spaces?
- What outdoor views do you want to capture (and avoid) from inside the sunroom?
- How will you access the room, from both outdoors and inside the house?

The goal here is to define your priorities and to think about how you will really use the space. Consider a few examples: If you like to bask in the sun while you read the paper with your morning coffee, your sunroom should have eastern exposure to capture the morning sunlight. If you like to sit and watch the sun go down in the evening, you'll want some western exposure (see Planning with the Sun, next page).

For those who wish to dine frequently in their sunroom, locating the space near the kitchen becomes an everyday convenience. Sunrooms that are used for entertaining or hanging out with friends should be easy to get to and have welcoming entrances, while sunrooms that provide peaceful seclusion should be less centrally located, and perhaps accessible only through a bedroom or other private space.

Depending on how it's integrated with the rest of the house, a sunroom can feel like one of the main rooms or, conversely, like a special retreat where you close the door to get away from it all. Creating a large opening into a sunroom brings light and warmth into adjacent rooms and allows for free traffic flow between spaces. For greater separation, French doors or sliding glass patio doors can provide a barrier without blocking too much light. Since sunrooms are weatherized and climate-controlled spaces, there's usually no need to separate them with standard entry doors. Most sunroom owners include a secure entry door on the sunroom only and use passage doors, if any, between the sunroom and the house.

The size of your lot is a factor when locating a sunroom. Zoning restrictions can vary depending on the location of the addition. For example, setback minimums may prohibit a sunroom on the front of a house but allow it on either side or at the back.

Continuous flooring and a large opening create a nearly seamless transition between this family room and the adjacent sunroom.

Used primarily as a garden room, this sunny space is clearly separated from the main living areas, providing a warm haven for both plants and people.

Planning with the Sun

While it may seem only natural that a sunroom should be located and designed for maximum exposure to the sun, this isn't always the best approach. Depending on where you live and how you plan to use your sunroom, you may want limited exposure during certain times of the day or year. In any case, it's important to consider the sun's movements and how it will reach your sunroom throughout the seasons.

Due to the earth's elliptical orbit, the sun's relative position in the sky changes from its high point (around June 21st) to its low point (around December 21st). The farther north you live from the equator, the lower the sun is in the sky, regardless of the time of year. Of course, the sun always rises in the east and sets in the west, so east-facing rooms get direct exposure in the early morning until near midday, while west-facing rooms get full sun in the late afternoon and evening. In North America, the north facade of a house receives no direct sun.

When architects design homes for passive solar heating, they typically orient the long side of the house toward the south and fill it with windows. There are two reasons for this. First, the south face of a house gets the most sun exposure every day of the year. More exposure means more light and more solar heat. Second, due to the variation in the sun's path, the interior of the house gets more sun in the winter, when it needs it most. In the summer, when the sun is highest in the sky, most of its rays are absorbed or blocked by the roof or window awnings, so less unwanted heat comes through the windows. These same design principles apply to sunrooms, provided they have a solid roof. South-facing structures with glass roofs get the maximum sun exposure every day of the year.

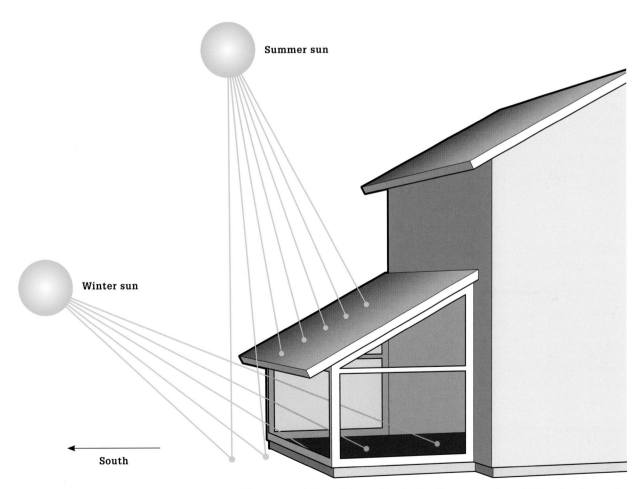

The sun's high angle in summer means more of its heat and direct light are blocked by the sunroom's roof. Extending the roof eave provides additional protection for south-facing windows. In winter, the sun's low angle allows rays to extend well into the sunroom's interior.

(continued)

Southern exposure and a concrete, stone, or tile floor is a winning combination for passive solar heating: the floor absorbs the sun's heat during the day and slowly releases it later as the temperature drops.

Skylights add welcome sunlight to a room, but also a considerable amount of heat. Use them judiciously to prevent excessive heat gain, and consider low-e glazing and/or heat-blocking shades.

All of this discussion leads to the important matter of heat gain, or how much your sunroom will heat up due to sun exposure. There are several ways to control heat gain, either to increase it or reduce it. Choosing windows with low-e coatings reduces heat gain without restricting too much light, while tinted windows keep the heat and glare down but also add color to your view. As shown in the illustration on page 171, shading provided by roof overhangs and window awnings helps block summer sun while letting winter rays through. This is a good technique if you want to maximize heat gain in the winter. Another traditional shading method is to plant large deciduous trees near the sunniest sides of the room. In summer, the leafed out trees provide heavy shade, while in winter, their bare branches let much of the sunlight through.

Regardless of the methods used to reduce heat gain, blocking the sun from the outside and preventing it from reaching the house is more effective than shading the windows from the inside. However, window shades remain the most common method for controlling excess heat and light in sunrooms. Unless your room will have very little southern and western exposure (western exposure is the worst for afternoon heat in the summer), you should plan to include quality window shades in your budget.

Finally, it's important to remember that while heat gain can be an ongoing challenge, it's better to have too much sun than to have too little. If you live in a climate with long winters, you'll be able to enjoy your sunroom in the colder, darker months—quite a luxury; not to mention, you'll save costs on heating for this space as well.

Construction Options

There are a handful of different ways you can go about building a new sunroom. The most popular option is to hire out the construction and/or installation to a professional builder or a firm that specializes in sunrooms. Among this group of pros, some specialize in custom projects, some work directly with manufacturers to install modular (prefabricated) sunrooms, and some do both custom and prefab work. Another option is to build the sunroom yourself using a do-it-yourself kit, which can save you a lot of money. However, unless a sunroom kit is made with insulated (double-pane) windows, it's probably not practical for year-round use in cold climates. And finally, if you have the inclination and the wherewithal, you can design and build your own custom sunroom, most likely over the course of many, many weekends.

CUSTOM SUNROOMS

A custom, site-built sunroom addition offers the ultimate in design flexibility. It's also the best way to ensure architectural continuity—that is, building something that looks like part of your original house. If your budget allows, a custom sunroom can include whatever you want, from a creative layout to a soaring cathedral ceiling to any door and window configuration that suits your home.

Custom sunrooms are typically built much like standard room additions, with wood-framed, insulated walls and roof. The exterior wall finish can be the same material as your house siding or it can introduce a different material that complements the facade's decorative scheme. The same goes for all interior finishes. As for the floor, a popular option for sunrooms is to pour a new concrete slab, which can be used as the finish flooring or be covered with other flooring materials. The floor can also be built as a standard wood-frame structure.

If you're in the market for a tailor-made sunroom, talk to several local contractors who specialize in projects similar to yours. Be sure to check out the quality of their work on other projects they've completed around town, and talk to those home-owners about their experiences with the contractors. Depending on the complexity of your plans, you might also want to hire an architect or a qualified designer for help with any or all stages of the design process. Most architects can also be retained to serve as a project manager or to oversee the construction phase of the job.

This shallow, two-story sunroom benefited from custom design and construction to take full advantage of the limited space available and to blend with the European styling of the home.

(continued)

Large yet well proportioned, this sunroom addition bears the marks of custom work in its unique, Asian-inspired details, like the extended roof eave and integrated gutter with rain chains in place of conventional downspouts.

MANUFACTURED SUNROOMS

As their name indicates, manufactured sunrooms (also called modular or prefab) are assembled from factory-made parts that are shipped to your home for quick installation by a trained crew. The advantage of manufactured rooms is that they are typically less expensive than custom creations, and the entire process, from planning to design to job completion, can take as little as a month or two. Prefab sunrooms are generally made with low-maintenance materials, like aluminum and vinyl, which makes them both durable and easy to care for. The downsides of this type of sunroom are limited design possibilities and finish options, and somewhat generic styling.

Most sunroom manufacturers operate through local dealers who offer turnkey service. After an in-home consultation with the customer, the dealer puts together a design for the room and offers a quote for the complete package. The final price typically includes all necessary preparation work, like pouring a foundation and a floor, as well as the installation. Product options vary by manufacturer; most offer high-performance windows and glazed roof panels as upgrade items, and some offer wood cladding instead of vinyl for the interior of frame members.

Because you're using the same company for virtually every aspect of the sunroom project, it pays to shop around for the right products and a reputable dealer who offers competitive pricing. Visit previous jobs of each prospective vendor, and talk to other customers about their satisfaction with the installation work and the sunroom products.

Manufactured sunrooms are all about construction efficiency, but it takes an experienced crew to complete the prep work, room assembly, and tie-in to the house.

DO-IT-YOURSELF SUNROOMS

Designed with simple, modular construction, do-it-yourself sunrooms are flat-packed and shipped to your door ready to assemble. The complete kits include roof panels, windows, screens, doors, and any extras that you order from the factory. In addition to the easy installation, one of the best features of this type of sunroom is its light weight. Thanks in part to their single-pane, non-glass panels and windows, sunroom kits are light enough to install right on top of patio slabs and wood decks.

For homes in colder climates, the non-insulated glazing is also the main disadvantage of D-I-Y sunrooms. Heating an essentially uninsulated room through the winter may not be a cost-effective or environmentally responsible option. As an alternative, you could thermally isolate the sunroom from the house during the coldest months, with an insulated wall and entry door. Then, during the cooler months of early spring and late fall, use the room with supplemental heating as needed.

Many DIY sunrooms can be installed on existing patios and decks, but make sure your installation is approved by the local building department, and be sure to have any supporting structure inspected by an engineer or qualified builder.

Building Elements

Whether you're building a new sunroom from scratch or adding on a manufactured room, there are plenty of decisions to make about what goes into the space, from structural and finish materials to how the room will be heated and cooled. The following is an overview of the basic building elements and some of the most popular options for different types of sunrooms.

FOUNDATION & FLOOR

All sunrooms must be built with a foundation that conforms to the local building code. The standard foundation consists of a concrete frost footing topped by a concrete or block foundation wall. Sunrooms built over decks are supported by the deck posts, which rest on (or are buried in) concrete piers that extend below the frost line. In warm climates, a slab-on-grade foundation may be permitted. This means that both the foundation and sunroom floor are created with a single, monolithic concrete slab.

Floor structures for sunrooms typically are concrete slabs or conventional lumber frames. Slabs are poured inside the foundation walls and can be finished to serve as the flooring material, if desired. Slabs are also ideal for in-floor radiant heating systems. Framed floors are built on top of the foundation walls, giving the floor a higher elevation and, if desired, allowing for a crawlspace beneath, convenient for running heating ducts, plumbing, wiring, and so forth. With some sunroom plans, you can also build floors with structural insulated panels, or SIPs.

When it comes to flooring materials, pretty much anything can work in a sunroom because the space is protected from the elements. Tile is clearly the most popular choice. Its appearance and durability are well suited to the indoor-outdoor feel and uses of a sunroom, and its water and stain resistance make it easy to care for plants without worrying about damage to the floor. Many types of tile—along with stone, brick, and bare concrete—are good for passive solar heating; they absorb and store heat from the sun during the day, then, when the sun goes down and the temperature drops, they release the heat slowly back into the air to help keep the room warm.

Concrete is another great flooring material for sunrooms and offers essentially the same benefits as tile. Thanks to the general popularity of concrete flooring, you can likely find local finishers and artisans who can perform decorative wonders on a plain, gray slab. Freshly poured floors can be dressed with inlays, embedded stone and glass, and a variety of textures and coloring techniques. Cured concrete can be acid-washed, stained, painted, or ground and polished.

Most types of conventional flooring are fine for sunrooms, depending, of course, on how you decorate and use the room. A word of warning: All that sunlight will quickly fade any material that isn't highly fade-resistant; and eventually, the sun fades everything. High-tech window coatings may help somewhat, but you shouldn't count on that for the long run. Also, if you like to keep the windows open and there's a good chance of getting rain inside, stay clear of flooring that's easily damaged by moisture, such as conventional carpet and some laminate flooring. If you have your heart set on carpet, consider modular carpet tiles. Available in a wide range of styles, carpet tiles come with their own backing and install in minutes. Best of all, if a tile gets especially dirty, it can be lifted up, washed in the sink, and set back into place.

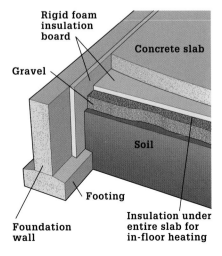

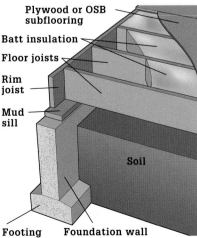

Floor types: Concrete slab floors (left) are insulated along their outside edges to prevent cold from migrating in from the foundation. Wood floors (right) are insulated in between each joist pair with fiberglass or other batt insulation.

Rigid foam insulation board
Concrete slab
Gravel
Soil
Footing
Foundation wall
Insulation under entire slab for in-floor heating

Plywood or OSB subflooring
Batt insulation
Floor joists
Rim joist
Mud sill
Soil
Footing
Foundation wall

WALLS

Walls in sunrooms can be framed conventionally, with 2 × 4s or 2 × 6s (2 × 6s are recommended because they leave more room for insulation), or with post-and-beam construction. Post-and-beam is a traditional framing technique using widely spaced lumber posts supporting heavy horizontal beams; this can be an efficient way to create large window openings. Most manufactured sunrooms are built with modified versions of post-and-beam framing with insulated panels for solid-wall infill. All sunroom walls should be well insulated for energy performance and to minimize solar heat gain through the walls.

You can finish the walls of a sunroom with anything you'd use in the rest of your house. But, as with flooring, be aware of the conditions. If moisture is a concern, either from rain coming in the windows or from high humidity, avoid drywall altogether or consider water or mold-resistant versions. And keep in mind the potential for fading before investing in wallpaper.

Structural Insulated Panels ▸

Made from two layers of oriented strandboard (OSB) sandwiched over a core of rigid insulation, SIPs are often used in sunrooms as an all-in-one system in place of conventional lumber framing, batt insulation, and sheathing. Sunroom manufacturers commonly use a variation of SIPs for their roof and wall panels. SIPs typically come in 4-ft.-wide panels, in custom lengths up to 28 ft. long, and can be used for building roofs, walls, and floors.

ROOF

Unless it's glazed, a sunroom roof is framed with lumber and insulated just like any other roof in a house. Ceilings can be framed in so they're flat or they can follow the roof line to create a cathedral ceiling. As with walls, any standard finish works for sunroom ceilings. For architectural continuity, a solid roof on a sunroom addition should have the same pitch, style, and trim detailing as the roof sections on the main house. Using the same roofing material also helps integrate the addition, so it looks like it's meant to be there.

In addition to drywall, sunroom walls can be finished with plaster, stucco, and wood paneling. Traditional beadboard, shown here, provides a durable, resilient finish with a classic "porch" feel.

(continued)

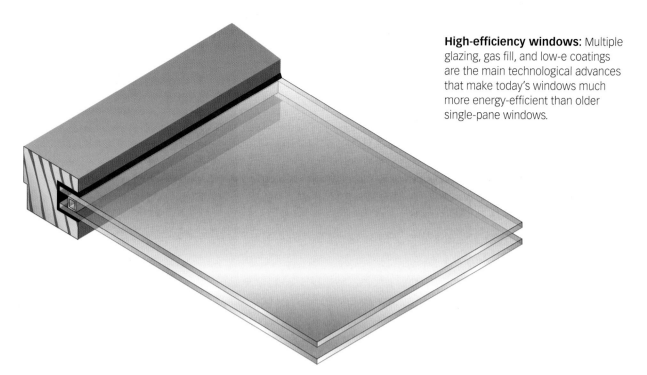

WINDOWS & DOORS

Because windows are so plentiful in sunrooms, choosing the right products is one of the most important decisions you can make. In general, the quality of the windows (also glazed doors, skylights, and roof windows) can make a big difference in the comfort and energy efficiency of the room year-round. Unless you live in a very warm climate or you plan to use your sunroom primarily as a three-season space (that is, you won't be heating it in winter), it's really not practical to use standard single-pane windows. Double-pane glazing can insulate two to four times better than single-pane, adding up to significant heating and cooling savings over the life of the windows.

High-performance windows are available in all types, styles, and sizes, while special coatings and other high-tech features allow you to tailor the windows' performance to suit your sunroom and the local climate. Here's a look at the main performance features to compare when shopping for new windows and other glazed products.

Glazing: All energy-efficient windows have at least two panes of glass to create an insulating dead-air space within the glazing. The sealed space between the panes impedes the transfer of heat and cold. Triple- and quadruple-glazed windows are also available, both of which may use a thin film of plastic in place of glass for one or more of the panes.

Gas Fill: Instead of a sealed air space between glazing panes, manufacturers often fill the space with a low-conductivity gas, which insulates better than air. Argon is the standard gas fill, while krypton or argon-krypton mixtures offer even better performance.

Edge Spacers: The spacer material used between multiple layers of glazing is critical to a window's performance and longevity. Spacers separate the glazing and seal in the air or gas fill between the panes. If this seal breaks, the air or gas escapes and fresh air and water vapor are allowed inside, leading to condensation (windows fogging from the inside) and greatly reducing the insulating quality of multiple panes. Common spacer materials include metal (aluminum or steel), silicone foam, butyl rubber, and vinyl. Because metal is a good heat conductor (bad for windows), these spacers should have a thermal break to minimize heat loss. Be sure to ask manufacturers about their warranties against seal failure, as a broken seal usually means the glazing must be replaced.

Low-E & Other Coatings: A low-e, or low-emissivity, coating is a super-thin, transparent metal film that lets light and heat in through the window but restricts heat going out. The same technology can be used to keep heat out of a sunroom in warmer climates where cooling is more important than heating. Tinted glazing is another way to reduce solar heat gain through windows. Better yet, tinted glass and tinting films cut down the heat with less darkening of the window for greater visibility.

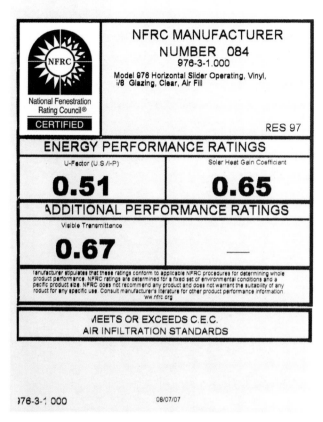

The official NFRC label carries the "CERTIFIED" NFRC logo and includes a description of the window or product line.

PERFORMANCE RATINGS

The primary industry authority that establishes performance ratings on new windows is the National Fenestration Rating Council (NFRC), a nonprofit group made up of window manufacturers, government agencies, and building trade associations. Look to the official NFRC label to compare performance ratings of various products and manufacturers. The two most important energy factors to consider are U-factor and solar heat gain coefficient (SHGC).

U-factor: The U-factor is a measure of how well a window insulates between hot and cold areas. NFRC tests for U-factor take into account the entire window—the glass, the glazing edges, and the window frame. The lower the U-factor, the better the window is at keeping heat in, or out of, the home.

Solar Heat Gain Coefficient: SHGC is a measure of how much solar heat a window lets in. Generally, sunrooms in cold climates should have windows with high SHGC, while rooms in hot climates are better with a lower SHGC. However, you may decide to fine-tune your windows' heat gain based on each window's location in the room (see Location-Specific Performance, below).

Additional Performance Ratings: Two other factors that may or may not be included on NFRC labels are visible transmittance and air leakage. The visible transmittance rating indicates how much light is allowed through a window. Clear-glass windows with minimal frame structures have higher visible transmittance ratings than tinted windows and those with more framing surrounding the glass area.

Air Leakage: This is self-explanatory. It's a measure of how much air can get through the window at joints where the sash meets the frame and other points of air infiltration. A non-operable picture window will have lower air leakage rating than a double-hung or slider window.

Location-Specific Performance: In some cases, it may make sense to choose different performance properties for specific areas of a sunroom. For example, on south-facing windows, you might specify premium low-e coatings and a high SHGC to take advantage of heat from the low winter sun, while east- and west-facing windows may have a lower SHGC to reduce unwanted heat gain in the summer. On the north side of a room, which tends to be the coldest, a low U-factor is most important. Talk with different manufacturers about the possibilities and potential extra costs of customizing your windows' glazing.

Resources for Window Information ▸

To help consumers make informed choices, the U.S. Department of Energy's Energy Star website (www.energystar.gov) includes a wealth of information on selecting windows for different weather zones. You can also find a list of manufacturers with Energy Star-qualified products, plus help with finding out about tax credits for purchasing high-performance windows. Other sources for window information include:

- NFRC: www.nfrc.org
- Efficient Windows Collaborative: www.efficientwindows.org
- American Architectural Manufacturers Association: www.aamanet.org
- Home Energy Magazine: www.homeenergy.org

(continued)

HEATING, COOLING & VENTILATION

Most sunrooms need some kind of mechanical heating and/or cooling to maintain comfortable temperatures throughout the year. In addition, providing for natural ventilation introduces fresh air and helps tame the heat during the warmer months. With all those windows, sunrooms can be difficult to heat and cool, but there are a number of effective methods you can employ. If you've chosen your windows carefully, you're more than halfway there, as the insulating quality of the glazing plays a significant role in the thermal properties of the room. After that, it's time to find the best mechanical systems to meet your needs.

Depending on the size of the sunroom and the capacity and configuration of your home's main heating/cooling system, you may be able to service the sunroom effectively by extending the existing network. Forced-air (furnace or heat pump) systems are extended by adding new supply and return ducts. Hydronic (boiler-based) systems are added onto with a new loop of hot-water piping and any related fixtures. In both cases, it's a good idea to set up the sunroom as a separate zone with its own thermostat. The temperature fluctuations in a sunroom tend to be more extreme than in the main parts of the house, and having direct control over the room offers convenience and greater energy efficiency. If expanding your existing system seems practical, hire a qualified HVAC (heating, ventilation, and air conditioning) contractor to come out and assess your situation.

You will also find a full range of supplemental heating systems that are well-suited to sunrooms and other additions. Among these, the easiest and least expensive to install are electric heaters, since they pretty much can go anywhere and some can be powered by a standard household circuit. Common electric heaters include baseboard units, radiant cove heaters, and through-the-wall heaters (which are typically also air conditioners). You can also heat your sunroom, while adding a touch of ambience with a direct-vent gas fireplace or a high-efficiency solid-fuel stove. In either case, look for products with good fuel efficiency and plenty of space-heating features, such as circulating fans, secondary heat exchangers, and variable temperature controls.

A ceiling fan is a low-cost and energy-efficient option for making your sunroom more comfortable in any weather.

Electric baseboard heaters are popular supplementary heat sources for porches and enclosed patios. They are inexpensive to purchase, relatively easy to install, and they can be independently controlled with wall-mounted or on-board thermostats. Look for a 240-volt model requiring a 20-amp or 30-amp circuit—they are much more efficient than 120-volt heaters.

As for cooling, many sunrooms are, at the least, equipped with the world's most basic mechanical cooling device: a ceiling fan. Ceiling fans don't lower the air temperature; they cool you by circulating air around your body, which in turn helps your body cool itself. Ceiling fans can also improve the effectiveness of both heating and cooling appliances. In the heating season, switch the fan's direction so it pushes air down, and set it on low speed. This takes the heated air that's trapped at the ceiling and moves it down into the room, which is especially helpful for sunrooms with high cathedral ceilings. Ceiling fans use very little energy compared to air conditioners, and they work in all climates.

But if a ceiling fan alone won't cut it, a room air conditioner or mini split heat pump can provide localized cooling with minimal setup work. Room air conditioners are commonly available in basic window-mount versions and through-the-wall units. The advantages of through-the-wall units are that they also provide heat, they are somewhat less visually obtrusive, and they don't occupy window space. The advantage of window units is that you can take them out at the end of each cooling season.

Mini split, or ductless, heat pumps also provide both heat and cooling power. These systems consist of an outdoor compressor/condenser unit and an indoor air-handling unit. The two units are connected by a conduit, which runs through the sunroom or house wall via a small (typically 3"-diameter) hole. The conduit can be quite long, allowing for considerable flexibility when locating both the indoor and outdoor units.

Sunrooms without adequate ventilation can quickly become stifling when the sun is out and all

that solar-heated air is trapped inside. The best way to provide for natural ventilation is with properly placed window and door openings. With the right setup, natural air convection will do all the work for you and ensure that the coolest available air comes in while the hottest air goes out.

Natural ventilation, or convection, is most simply explained by the rule that hot air rises and cold air drops. If you open windows in your basement and in the top floor of your house, you will establish a constant flow of air that brings cooler air in through the basement windows and ejects warmer air out through the upper floor windows. This effect, known as stack ventilation, works just the same in sunrooms. Operable windows placed near the floor draw in cooler air, which then rises through the room as it heats up, then leaves through window openings near the ceiling or, better yet, through operable skylights. A ventilation fan can produce the same effect, in lieu of upper windows or skylights.

Cross-ventilation allows for air movement in a different way. With windows or doors open on two or more sides of a sunroom, or in the sunroom and a nearby room in the house, air that's already blowing around outside is allowed to flush through your living space. The practice of opening windows to let air in is not new to anyone, of course, but it's important to keep in mind that cross-ventilation is most effective when windows can be opened on opposing sides of a room. If summer cooling is your primary objective, try to locate operable windows on an east- or north-facing wall of your sunroom, which can help pull in cooler air in the evenings when western-facing walls are especially hot.

Sun Porch

A sun porch, a sunroom, a three-season porch, a greenhouse, a hothouse, an orangerie, a conservatory… these names are not precisely interchangeable but all refer to a similar type of room. The common element all types share is that their walls and usually their roofs are made of clear panel glazing that allows light in and traps it, raising the ambient room temperature to more comfortable levels in cooler times of year. Some of these structures are designed for gardening-related activities; others are meant for enjoyment or entertainment. Some are freestanding, others are attached to a house.

If it is custom-built for you by a professional contractor, a sunroom can be quite expensive. But there is another option: a sunroom in a box. You can have a complete, do-it-yourself sunroom kit delivered to your home in cardboard boxes. A good deal of assembly is required, of course, but … with a few basic tools and a helper, most people with basic DIY skills can complete the job in a weekend.

The key features of this sun porch (manufactured by SunPorch Structures Inc., see Resources page 234) are its easy installation and its versatility. First, it's designed to install right on top of an existing concrete patio slab or a wood deck, eliminating the extensive site-prep work required with a custom project. If you don't have a patio or deck in place, you can build an inexpensive foundation with landscape timbers to support the sunroom structure, then create a floor inside using brick pavers, stone, wood decking tiles, or other suitable material. The sunroom manufacturer and your local building department can help you with the planning and construction details.

The sunroom's versatility is apparent in both its design and use. Its modular construction allows you to specify the height, width, and length of the structure to fit your needs and your house. Other modifications can be made at the factory to accommodate special installation requirements, such as installing the room to fit against the roof eave of your house or even slightly above the eave. The standard room design includes two matching end walls and a front wall. If your sunroom will fit into a corner where two house walls meet, simply order the room without one of the end walls. The sizes of end walls also can be adjusted to fit other house configurations.

Operable and removable windows make this sunroom versatile to use. In cooler months, all the windows can be closed against the cold to keep the sun's heat inside. As the weather warms up, you can open either the top or bottom window sash to capture the breezes. And in the summer, you can take the windows out completely to convert the sunroom into a fully screened patio room.

Check In With Your Building Department ▶

It's up to you to gain legal approval for your sunroom project. Contact your city's building department to learn what its rules are. Some municipalities require permits and inspections for DIY sunrooms, while others exclude structures that are installed over existing patios or decks and do not change the home's footprint. In any case, you should also consult with a qualified building professional to make sure your patio, deck, or other foundation can safely support a sunroom.

A DIY sunroom kit comes with all of the parts precut and predrilled for your own custom design. Assembling the kit is a relatively easy task that most couples can accomplish in a weekend.

Commercial-grade, lightweight glazing, and predrilled aluminum frame parts are the key components that make this sunroom kit lightweight and durable enough for shipping and also easy to assemble. Sunrooms can be perfectly acceptable spaces for evening activities, if you equip them with light fixtures (left).

Sun Porch Kit Accessories

Skylight shades give you control over light and heat coming through the roof panels. These 2-in-1 shades have a solid reflective panel that blocks most of the sun's light and heat and a translucent panel that blocks only half of the sunlight to reduce glare and heat gain while letting light filter through.

Precisely fitted wall shades are convenient for reducing glare and heat gain right where you need it. They're also great for adding privacy when and where you want it without blocking all of your sunroom views.

Optional roof vents allow hot air to escape and help to flush the interior of the sunroom with fresh air. Adjustable covers let you control the rate of air flow. The opening and closing mechanism is easy to operate from inside the sunporch.

Options for Attaching a Sun Porch to Your House

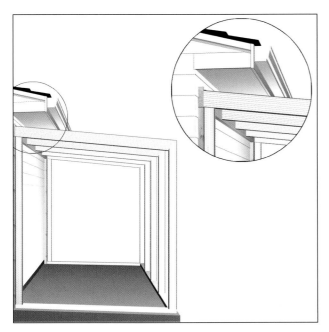

Attach the ledger directly to the wall if there is no eave overhang or if there is at least 6" of clear working space between the top of the ledger and the bottom of the eaves.

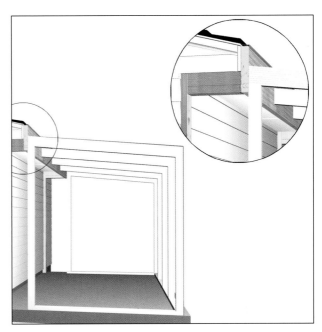

If the maximum height of the sun porch brings it up against or within 6" of the bottom of the eave overhang, extend the fascia on the eave downward and fill in with boards or siding between the cornice and the back post for the sun porch.

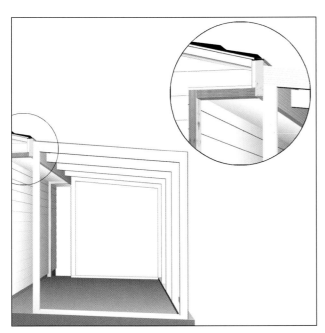

The ledger for the sun porch can be attached directly to the fascia board as long as the highest point of the sun-porch roof remains slightly lower than the roof covering. Be sure to attach the ledger so the lag screws hit into the ends of the rafter tails.

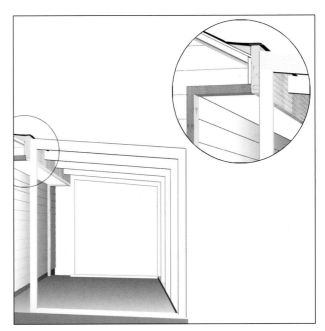

If the sun porch is slightly taller than the roof eaves, you can add a ledger that's taller than the fascia, but it cannot extend more than a couple of inches higher. Fill in the open area beneath the roof covering created at the side using a full-width wood wedge and caulk. The roof covering must retain a slight slope with no swales.

Preparing the Installation Site

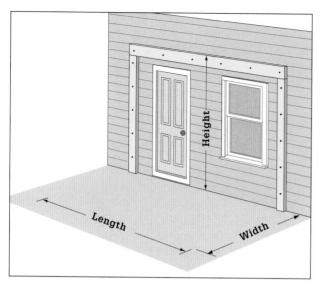

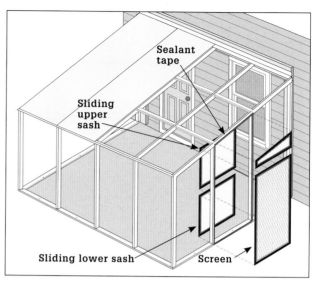

When attaching a sun porch directly to your exterior wall, install 2 × 6 or 2 × 8 edges and hang the roof support beams from it. Also install 2 × 4 vertical nailers beneath the ends of the edges for attaching the walls to the house. Ledgers also may be mounted to rafter ends in the eave area (see previous page).

Sun porch kits with non-glass panels can be mounted on practically any hard surface because they are light enough that they do not require a reinforced floor. You do need to make sure the floor is level, however (see next page), and that the base channels you lay out create square corners.

The Benefits of Roof Ventilation

Without roof vents, hot air is trapped in the sunroom, making it uncomfortable for users and inhospitable to plants.

A single roof vent creates an escape route for hot air, allowing you to regulate the temperature and keep the room cooler during hot weather. Multiple roof vents increase the ventilation efficiency, but increase the chances for leaks.

Options for Anchoring a Sun Porch

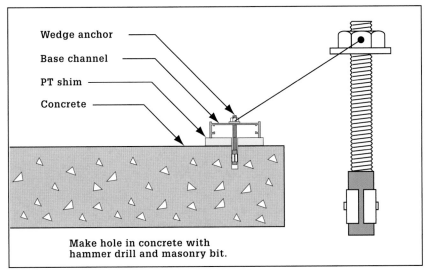

Wedge anchor
Base channel
PT shim
Concrete

Make hole in concrete with hammer drill and masonry bit.

On concrete patios, attach the base channel to the concrete surface with masonry anchors. There are many styles of anchors you can use. The hardware shown here is a wedge anchor that is driven into a hole drilled through the base channel and into the concrete. If your concrete slab is not level, you'll need to insert shims underneath the base channel in low spots.

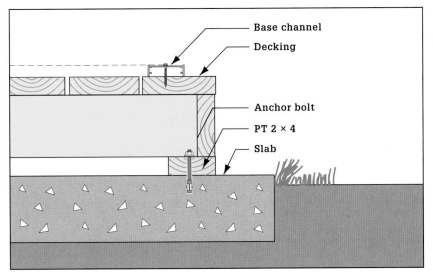

Base channel
Decking
Anchor bolt
PT 2 × 4
Slab

Building a new ground-level deck is a good way to create a stable floor for your sun porch if your concrete patio is in poor condition or if there is no other floor structure in the installation area. Attach pressure-treated 2 × 4 sleepers to the concrete surface to create a raised surface to set the deck on.

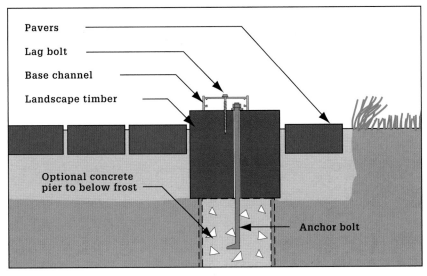

Pavers
Lag bolt
Base channel
Landscape timber
Optional concrete pier to below frost
Anchor bolt

Set treated wood timbers onto a concrete footing for a sturdy wall base that you can attach to directly when installing the base channels. The footings should extend below your frost line to keep the structure from shifting, but you can use a less permanent floor system, such as sand-set pavers, if you wish.

Tools & Materials

4-ft. level
Drill and bits
¼" and ⅜" hex nut drivers
#2 square screw (Robertson) bit
Socket wrench set
Chalk line
Caulking gun
Rubber mallet

Pressure-treated 2 × 4 and 2 × 6 lumber
Exterior house paint
Metal roof flashing
100% silicone caulk
¼" × 1½" and ¼" × 2½" corrosion-resistant lag screws
    and washers
Additional fasteners for securing sunroom to house
    and supporting surface

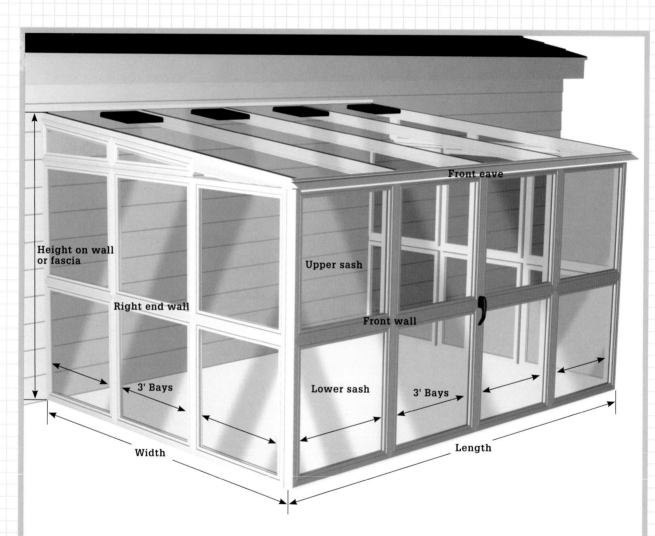

Sun Porch Terms

Mounting surface: May be a level wood deck,
    concrete slab or patio.
Right and left end walls: Reference point is with
    your back to the house looking outwards.
Kneewall (not shown): A site built wall used to
    increase the height of the structure.

Door Information

Door (included with kit) may be mounted in any
    front or end wall bay.
Door opening is 33" wide and 72" high.
Door swings outward and can be hinged for
    left-hand or right-hand operation.

How to Build a Sun Porch Kit

Install pressure-treated 2 x 4 vertical support cleats and a 2 × 6 horizontal support ledger onto the house wall, following the manufacturer's specifications (See page 187 for options). On non-lap siding, mount the support pieces directly over the siding. For lap siding, cut away the siding and mount the ledger and support cleats over the wall sheathing and building paper. Paint the ledger and cleats before installation, and add roof flashing over the header, leaving it unfastened until the sunroom roof is completely assembled. Make sure the ledger is perfectly level and the vertical cleats are plumb.

Countering Slope ▸

Make sure the wood deck, patio, or other installation base is level before installing the sunroom. If not, you may need to install long wood wedges that fit under the floor plates or take other corrective measures as suggested in your installation manual.

Pressure-treated shims

Tape

Base channel

Level

Lay out the base channel pieces onto your surface in the installation area. Join the pieces using the provided splice brackets and screws.

(continued)

3

Position the free ends of the base channel against the wall cleats. Use a 4-ft. level to make sure the channel sections are level. If necessary, use tapered shims to level the channel. Then, check the base frame for square by measuring diagonally from corner to corner. Make adjustments as needed until the measurements are equal.

4

Fasten the base frame to the surface using a recommended fastener at each of the predrilled mounting holes. Apply a bead of silicone caulk where the channel meets the surface on both sides of the channel. Install the base channel vertical brackets to the base channels using the provided screws (inset photo). These brackets will join the vertical end-wall tubes and front-wall columns to the base channel frame.

5

To begin assembling the wall and roof structures, first join the end-wall headers (the two outside rafters) and the rafters (the interior rafters) to the front-wall columns using the provided mounting brackets and screws. Also install the mounting brackets onto the free ends of the headers and rafters; these are used to mount the headers and rafters to the 2 × 6 support ledger (per step 1 on page 189) on the house wall.

6

Complete the end-wall assemblies by joining the vertical wall tubes to the end-wall headers using the provided hardware. Finally, install the mullion brackets onto the sides of the rafters and end-wall headers; these will join the horizontal mullions to the rafters and headers to tie the roof frame together (see Step 11).

7

With a helper, raise one of the end-wall assemblies into position and set the vertical tubes over the base channel brackets. Fasten the tubes to the brackets with screws. Install the other end-wall assembly the same way.

8

Anchor the end-wall assemblies to the 2 × 4 support cleats and the 2 × 6 support ledger on the house wall. Use a level to position the vertical tubes perfectly plumb, and secure the tubes to the cleats using the recommended fasteners driven through the predrilled holes. Secure the end-wall headers to the 2 × 6 support header using the recommended fasteners.

(continued)

9

Snap a chalk line across the face of the 2 × 6 support ledger so the line is flush with the tops of the end-wall headers. This line corresponds to the tops of the rafters and the bottom edge of the top mullion pieces.

10

Working from one end wall to the other, position the first rafter-front column assembly in place, and secure the column to the base channel using the provided screws. Then, install the horizontal mullions between the end-wall header and the first rafter using the provided screws. Repeat this process to install the remaining rafter assemblies and mullions.

11

Install the top mullion pieces: Apply silicone caulk to the 2 × 6 support ledger to seal the vertical flange of the top mullions to the ledger. Also caulk where the horizontal flanges of the mullions will meet the end-wall headers and rafters. Working from the right end wall to the left, secure the top mullions to the end-wall headers and the rafters using the provided screws.

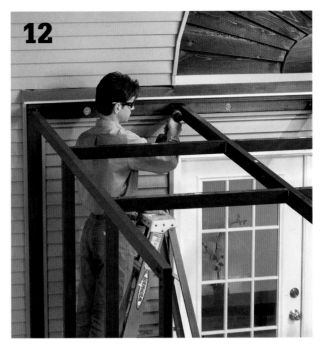

12

Anchor the rafters to the 2 × 6 support ledger using the recommended fasteners driven through the mounting brackets you installed on the rafter ends in Step 6.

13

Install the header caps over the tops of the end-wall headers; these will help secure the roof glazing panels. First apply a bead of caulk down the center of each header, stopping it 3" from the end of the header. Set each cap into the wet caulk and secure it with the provided screws. Install the rafter caps following the same procedure.

14

Install the eave mullions over the exposed ends of the rafters and end-wall headers. Apply caulk over the center of each frame part and around each predrilled hole. Set the mullions into the wet caulk and secure them with screws. *Note: Complete all additional caulking of the framing as recommended by the manufacturer.*

(continued)

Prepare the roofing panels for installation by taping the ends: Cover the top end of each panel with a strip of aluminum tape, and cover the bottom end with vented tape; both tapes are provided. Follow the manufacturers instructions to install any optional roof vents.

Apply adhesive foam gasket strips (provided) to the roof battens that will secure the glazing panels to the roof framing, following the manufacturer's directions. Be careful not to pull or stretch the gaskets. Also apply gaskets to the roof framing, along the end-wall headers, rafters, top mullions, and eave mullions, as directed.

Remove the protective film from the first roofing panel, making sure the UV-protected side of the panel is facing up. With a helper, place the panel on top of the end-wall header and the adjacent rafter at one end of the roof. The panel should rest against the eave mullion along the front wall.

Secure the outside edge and ends of the panel with the appropriate battens, using the provided screws. To fasten battens to the eave mullion, first drill pilot holes into the mullion, using the predrilled batten holes as a guide. Carefully caulk the panel and battens at the prescribed locations.

Position the next roofing panel onto the rafters, and secure it with battens. The long, vertical batten covers both long edges of the first two panels. *Tip: You have to reach across a panel to fasten vertical battens. This is easiest when you have a tall ladder and use a magnetic nut driver on your drill, which allows you to drive the screws with one hand.* Complete the flashing details along the 2 × 6 roof header as directed.

Install the remaining roofing panels, following the same procedure. Be sure to caulk the roofing carefully at all prescribed locations.

(continued)

21

Begin the wall section installation by adding a triangular aluminum filler piece to the front section of each end wall. Install the fillers with the provided brackets and screws, then caulk along the top and ends of the fillers as directed.

22

Apply sealant tape along the perimeter of the first section on the front wall. Press the strips of tape firmly together to create a seal at each corner. *Tip: Storing the roll of tape in the refrigerator prior to installation makes it easier to work with.*

Tip ▶

The sunroom's door can go into any one of the wall sections. When choosing the location, plan for easy access to both the house and yard. Also consider how the sunroom's layout will be affected by traffic flow into and out of the door. The door itself always opens out, but it can be hinged on either the right or left side.

23

Determine the door location (see Tip, previous page). Install the first screen/window frame: Set the panel onto the base channel, making sure the frame's weep holes are at the bottom. Align the frame within the opening, and press inward firmly to seat it into the sealant tape. Secure the frame with the provided screws. Install the remaining frames using the same techniques.

24

Install the trapezoidal windows under the headers on the end walls: Apply sealant tape as before, position the window, then secure it with the provided screws.

(continued)

25

Complete the window installation by removing the bottom and top sash of each window frame. Peel off the protective film from the glazing, then reinstall each sash, following the manufacturer's directions.

26

Begin the door installation by fastening the door threshold to the base channel, using the provided screws. Then, add the weatherstripping to the hinge bar and latch bar pieces and the header piece. Trim the excess weatherstripping.

27

Decide which side of the door will be hinged. Align the hinge bar (with door attached) to the markings on the vertical wall tube or front column, drill pilot holes, and mount the door to the column with screws.

28

29

Install the latch bar, leaving a ⅛" gap between the bar and the door edge. Install the header piece, also with a ⅛" gap. Complete the door assembly to add the handle, sweep, and closer, following the manufacturer's instructions.

Apply sealant tape to the door frame, and install the two glazing panels as directed. Add the decorative cover on each side of the door, seating it with a rubber mallet. If the door is located on one of the end walls, install the trapezoidal window above the door, using the same techniques described in Step 24.

Low-Maintenance Sunroom

The term "sunroom" can refer to many different types of rooms, from conservatory-style networks of metal frames and glazing that covers the roof as well as the walls to just about any room in your house that has banks of windows to introduce direct sunlight. The sunroom shown in this project (see Resources, p. 235) is a three-season porch that encloses a second-story walk-out deck. The room is a modular kit that was custom-fabricated to the homeowner's exact design and then assembled on site. Except for some custom framing work where the rooflines intersect, the installation was accomplished in a single day.

Built from rigid PVC panels that fit into aluminum frames, this sunroom measures 14 ft. by 14 ft. with a 10-ft. gable peak. The sidewalls are 7 ft. high. The underlying deck area is covered with plywood sheathing that will become a substrate for the finished floor—here, vinyl tiles. The glazing on the windows of the room is a clear vinyl fabric that can stretch to absorb impact and accommodate seasonal changes in framework dimensions.

The installers featured in this project are professional carpenters contracted by the sunroom seller. Custom sunrooms such as this can be ordered and installed by do-it-yourselfers as well. As a percentage of the total package price you won't save a lot by doing the labor yourself, however.

Although they are not seen in the photos, a number of electrical receptacles were installed in the sunroom floor. The feeder cables run back to the house through conduit in the deck joist cavities, because the solid foam panels in the walls and ceilings do not readily accept cables.

Tools & Materials ▸

Drill/driver
Circular saw
Reciprocating saw
Tape measure
Caulk gun
Level
Utility knife
Custom wall panels
Custom doors
    with latches
Ceiling panels
Aluminum floor track
Aluminum vertical
    wall track
Aluminum upper
    wall track

Roof I-beams
Three-part ridge
    pole support
Ridge pole
    (engineered beam)
Snap-in fascia
Snap-in gutter with
    downspouts
Moisture-resistant
    floor covering
Roof covering (shingles)
Framing lumber
Weatherproof silicone
    sealant
Hex-head screws
    (1", 2", 7")

To prepare for this new sunroom addition, an old deck was replaced with a new, beefier model. It features a sturdy staircase with enough room on the left side of the addition for an open-air grilling area that is accessed through a door in the sunroom. Instead of decking, the deck area in the sunroom installation area is covered with ¾" tongue-in-groove plywood sheathing.

BEFORE

Low-Maintenance Sunroom Kit Parts

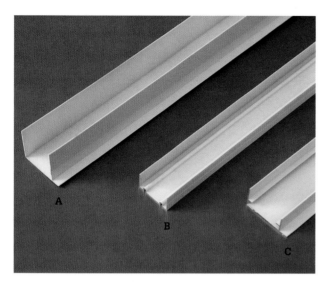

Aluminum tracks secure the prefabricated wall panels. Shown are sections of floor track (A), vertical wall track (B) and upper wall track (C).

Fasteners for this sunroom include: self-tapping hex-head screws (1") with low-visibility white heads (A), insulation screws (7") with 2"-dia. fender washers (B), and galvanized self-tapping hex-head screws (2") with self-sealing EPDM rubber washers (C).

Wall panels for sunroom kits consist of rigid PVC frames with foam insulation in the core. The window sash telescopes downward in four tracks to provide maximum ventilation when open.

Clear vinyl glazing stretches under impact and will not shatter or crack. It is also light enough in weight that sunroom kits often can be installed without structural reinforcement that may be required for units with glass-glazed windows.

Roof panels come in varying thicknesses depending on the thickness of the rigid foam insulation board that is used (here, 4"). The narrow filler panel seen here features washable PVC beadboard on the interior side to create a ready-to-go ceiling once it is installed. The exterior side of the panel is ⅝" oriented strand board (OSB) to create a surface for installing building paper and asphalt shingles.

How to Install a Low-Maintenance Sunroom

1

PVC flashing (isolation)

Install the aluminum floor track channels at the perimeter of the installation area. Use a bead of weatherproof silicone sealant and self-tapping, 2" hex-head screws with EPDM rubber washers to secure the track. Square layout lines should be marked prior to installation. If your plywood substrate layer is treated with ACQ or copper azole wood treatment, protect the aluminum tracks from corrosion by installing an isolation layer of PVC flashing (sold in rolls).

2

Prepare the house walls for installation of the vertical wall tracks. Mark a cutting line on the siding at the track location and remove siding so you can fasten the tracks to the wall sheathing. *Tip: Use a cordless trim saw with a standard blade installed backward to cut vinyl siding.*

3

Remove gutters and other obstructions from the installation area. The exact requirements for this step depend on the configuration of your roof and how you will be tying into the roofline or wall to make space for the sunroom roof.

4

Install the vertical wall track channels with silicone sealant and self-sealing screws. If the wall sheathing will not accept screws and is not backed by plywood sheathing, you will need to install sturdy wood or wood sheathing backers to secure the track.

(continued)

Install the first wall panel. In many cases, the first panel will be a narrow filler strip that is simply a solid wall panel and does not contain windows. Install the panel by driving 1" self-tapping screws through the floor track flanges and into the bottom frame of the panel. Make sure the panel is plumb and firmly seated against the track.

Add the next panel according to the installation sequence diagram that comes with your kit. Make sure the panel is plumb and then tack it into position by driving self-tapping screws through the floor flange. The panels lock together at the edges, which will hold them temporarily until the upper wall track can be installed. If you are working in windy conditions, you may need to brace the panels.

Filler panel

Corner post

Install a corner post at the first corner. The flange on the side of the L-shaped post (inset photo) should capture the end of the first wall's last wall panel. The second wall's first wall panel will fit into the other leg of the L.

Upper wall track

Fit the upper wall track over the entire first wall after cutting it to length. The end of the track that joins with the track on the next wall should be mitered to make a neat joint. If the adjoining wall is gabled, this will mean making a relatively tricky compound miter cut. Refer to your plan for the exact angle and don't be shy about asking for help.

Continue installing panels on the second wall. If it is a gabled wall, install panels up to the midpoint; then cut the three-part, ridge pole support post to fit, and install it by driving screws through the post and into the wall panel. Make sure the saddle formed at the top of the post is sized to accept the ridge pole.

Install the remaining wall panels, creating corners and adding upper wall tracks as you go. Frequently check for plumb and level, and make sure all panels are seated firmly in the tracks.

Mark the upper wall tracks at the gable for cutting by transferring the edges of the ridge pole saddle onto the ends of tracks. Cut them to length and the correct angle with a power miter saw and metal cutting blade. Or, you can use an old combination blade that you don't mind making dull.

Set the ridge pole into the saddle in the ridge pole post, and adjust it until the overhang is correct. Check the length: if the pole does not end at the correct point on the other end, re-cut it or adjust your overhang amount. Secure the end by driving screws through the ridge pole post and into the ridge pole.

(continued)

Ridge pole

Wall cap plate

Secure the house-end of the ridge pole. Begin by installing a temporary post near the house wall that is the same height as the bottom of the saddle opening in the ridge pole post. Make sure the ridge pole is level and then measure for attaching it to the house. The exact method you use depends on the house structure. Here, the exterior wall that will support the ridge is set back 18" from a pair of bay windows that are covered by the same roof. This means that the cap plate for the bearing wall that will support the ridge pole is lower than the bottom of the pole. The distance is measured (left photo) and a 2 x 6 half-lap post anchor is constructed. The anchor is nailed to the cap plate on the wall and then the ridge pole is attached to the anchor with deck screws (right photo).

Begin installing roof panels. The full-width panels seen here are 4-ft. wide, yet they are strong enough to meet minimum dead load ("snow") requirements even in cold climates. The panels are attached with long insulation screws that are fitted with fender washers and driven into the ridge pole and upper wall track.

I-beam

Install I-beams on the roof next to the first roof panel. The track on one side of the I-beam should capture the leading edge of the first roof panel. Attach the I-beam to the roof panel with self-tapping screws driven through the I-beam flange and down into the OSB panel surface.

16

Add the next roof panel to the roof, sliding it into the open side of the I-beam. Square the panel with the roof, and then drive insulation screws down through the panel and into the ridge pole and the upper wall track. Add the next I-beam and fasten it with self-tapping screws.

17

Continue installing panels and I-beams until the roof is complete. Complete one full side before beginning the other.

18

Gutter

Install fascia and gutters. The materials seen here are designed specifically to work with the roof panel system of this kit. The fascia snaps over the ends of the roof panels and is secured with screws. The gutters fit into tracks on the fascia and are secured with screws.

19

Install the prehung doors by fastening the door nailing flanges to the frames that create the door opening. Make sure the door is level and plumb before driving fasteners. Attach the door handle and latch.

20

Make finishing touches, such as trimming off excess insect screening and painting or cladding the ridge pole. If your sunroom does not have a finished ceiling, add one (tongue-and-groove cedar carsiding is a good choice). Install floorcoverings.

Hard-sided Greenhouse Kit

Building a greenhouse from a prefabricated kit offers many advantages. Kits are usually very easy to assemble because all parts are prefabricated and the lightweight materials are easy to handle. The quality of greenhouse kits varies widely, though, and buying from a reputable manufacturer will help ensure that you get many years of service from your greenhouse.

If you live in a snowy climate, you may need to either provide extra support within the greenhouse or be ready to remove snow whenever there is a significant snowfall because the lightweight aluminum frame members can easily bend under a heavy load. Before buying a kit, make sure to check on how snowfall may affect it.

Greenhouse kits are offered by many different manufacturers, and the exact assembly technique you use will depend on the specifics of your kit. Make sure you read the printed instructions carefully, as they may vary slightly from this project.

The kit we're demonstrating here is made from aluminum frame pieces and transparent polycarbonate panels and is designed to be installed over a base of gravel about 5" thick. Other kits may have different base requirements.

When you purchase your kit, make sure to uncrate it and examine all the parts before you begin. Make sure all the pieces are there and that there are no damaged panels or bent frame members.

A perfectly flat and level base is crucial to any greenhouse kit, so make sure to work carefully. Try to do the work on a dry day with no wind, as the panels and frame pieces can be hard to manage on a windy day. Never try to build a greenhouse kit by yourself. At least one helper is mandatory, and you'll do even better with two or three.

Construction of a greenhouse kit consists of four basic steps: laying the base, assembling the frame, assembling the windows and doors, and attaching the panels.

Greenhouse kits come in a wide range of shapes, sizes, and quality. The best ones have tempered-glass glazing and are rather expensive. The one pictured here is glazed with corrugated polyethylene and is at the low end of the cost spectrum.

The familiar gambrel profile is tricky to create from scratch, but when purchased as a kit a gambrel greenhouse is a snap to assemble.

Some greenhouse kits include only the hardware necessary to create the frame structure. The glazing, which is normally some variety of plastic sheeting, is acquired separately.

Kit greenhouses (and other types, too) can be built in groups so you may create a variety of growing climates. This lets you raise species that may not have compatible needs for light, moisture and heat.

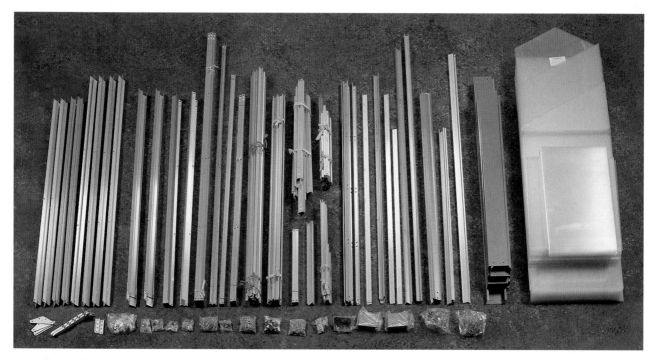

Organize and inspect the contents of your kit cartons to make sure all of the parts are present and in good condition. Most manuals will have a checklist. Staging the parts makes for a more efficient assembly. Be sure not to leave any small parts loose, and do not store parts in high-traffic areas.

A cordless drill/driver with a nut-driver accessory will trim hours off of your assembly time compared with using only hand tools.

Rent outdoor power equipment if you need to do significant regrading to create a flat, level building base. Be sure to have your local utility company inspect for any buried utility lines first. (You may prefer to hire a landscaping company to do re-grading work for you.)

How to Build a Greenhouse Kit

Create an outline for the base of the greenhouse using stakes and string. The excavation should be about 2" wider and longer than the overall dimensions of your greenhouse. To ensure that the excavation is perfectly square, measure the diagonals of the outline. If diagonals are equal, the outline is perfectly square. If not, reposition the stakes until the outline is square.

Excavate the base area to a depth of 5". Use a long 2 × 4 and a 4-ft. level to periodically check the excavation and to make sure it is level and flat. You can also use a laser level for this job.

Assemble the base of the greenhouse using the provided corner connectors and end connectors, attaching them with base nuts and bolts. Lower the base into the excavation area, and check to make sure it's level. Measure the diagonals to see if they are equal; if not, reposition the base until the diagonals are equal, which ensures that the base is perfectly square. Pour a layer of gravel or other fill material into the excavation to within about 1" of the top lip of the base frame. Smooth the fill with a long 2 × 4.

(continued)

4

Bottom wall plate

Base

Attach the bottom wall plates to the base pieces so that the flanged edges face outside the greenhouse. In most systems, the floor plates will interlock with one another, end to end, with built-in brackets.

5

Corner stud

Fasten the four corner studs to the bottom wall plates using hold-down connectors and bolts. In this system, each corner stud is secured with two connectors.

6

Side ceiling plate

Front ceiling plate

Assemble the pieces for each side ceiling plate, then attach one assembled side plate against the inside of the two corner studs, making sure the gutter is positioned correctly. Now attach the front ceiling plate to the outside of the two corner studs that are over the front floor plate.

Backward and Forward ▶

With some kits you need to go backward to go forward. Because the individual parts of your kit depend upon one another for support, you may be required to tack all the parts together with bolts first and then undo and remake individual connections as you go before you can finalize them. For example, in this kit you must undo the track/brace connections one at a time so you can insert the bolt heads for the stud connectors into the track.

Attach the other side ceiling plate along the other side, flat against the inside of the corner studs. Then attach corner brackets to the rear studs, and construct the back top plate by attaching the rear braces to the corners and joining the braces together with stud connectors.

Corner bracket

Stud connectors

Fasten the left and right rear studs to the outside of the rear floor plate, making sure the top ends are sloping upward, toward the peak of the greenhouse. Attach the center rear studs to the rear floor plate, fastening them to the stud connectors used to join the rear braces.

Attach the side studs on each side wall using the provided nuts and bolts. Then attach the doorway studs to the front wall of the greenhouse.

Doorway studs

(continued)

10

Attach diagonal struts as specified by the manufacturer. Periodically take diagonal measurements between the top corners of the greenhouse, adjusting as necessary so that the measurements are equal and the greenhouse is square.

11

Fasten the gable-end stud extensions to the front and back walls of the greenhouse. The top ends of the studs should angle upward toward the peak of the greenhouse.

12

Assemble the roof frame on a flat area near the wall assembly. First assemble the crown-beam pieces; then attach the rafters to the crown, one by one. The end rafters, called the crown beams, have a different configuration, so make sure not to confuse them.

Rafter

Crown

Crown beam

With at least one helper, lift the roof into place onto the wall frames. The gable-end studs should meet the outside edges of the crown beams, and the ends of the crown beams rest on the outer edge of the corner bracket. Fasten in place with the provided nuts and bolts.

Side braces

Roof support window

Attach the side braces and the roof support window beams to the underside of the roof rafters as specified by the manufacturer's instructions.

Attach the front braces between the corner studs and the doorway studs on the front wall of the greenhouse.

(continued)

Build the roof windows by first connecting the two side window frames to the top window frame. Slide the window panel into the frame; then secure it by attaching the bottom window frame. Slide the window into the slot at the top of the roof crown; then gradually lower it in place. Attach the window stop to the window support beam.

Assemble the doors, making sure the top slider/roller bar and the bottom slider bar are correctly positioned. Lift the door panels up into place onto the top and bottom wall plates.

Install the panels one-by-one using panel clips. Begin with the large wall panels. Position each panel and secure it by snapping a clip into the frame at the intervals specified by the manufacturer's instructions.

Add the upper panels. At the gable ends, the upper panels will be supported by panel connectors that allow the top panel to be supported by the bottom panel. The lower panels should be installed already.

Install the roof panels and roof-window panels so that the top edges fit up under the edge of the crown or window support and the bottom edges align over the gutters.

Test the operation of the doors and roof windows to make sure they operate smoothly.

Appendix: Construction Tips

The wide variety of nail styles and sizes makes it possible to choose exactly the right fastener for each job. Nails are identified by their typical purpose, such as casing, flooring, or roofing nails; or by a physical feature, such as galvanized, coated, or spiral. Some nails come in both a galvanized and non-galvanized version. Use galvanized nails for outdoor projects and non-galvanized indoors. Nail lengths may be specified in inches or by numbers from 4 to 60 followed by the letter "d," which stands for "penny" (see "Nail Sizes," opposite page).

Some of the most popular nails for carpentry projects include:

- Common and box nails for general framing work. Box nails are smaller in diameter, which makes them less likely to split wood. Box nails were designed for constructing boxes and crates, but they can be used in any application where thin, dry wood will be nailed close to the edge of the piece. Most common and box nails have a cement or vinyl coating that improves their holding power.

- Finish and casing nails, that have small heads and are driven just below the work surface with a nail set. Finish nails are used for attaching moldings and other trim to walls. Casing nails are used for nailing window and door casings. They have a slightly larger head than finish nails for better holding power.

- Brads, small wire nails sometimes referred to as finish nails. They are used primarily in cabinetry, where very small nail holes are preferred.

- Flooring nails, that are often spiral-shanked for extra holding power to prevent floorboards from separating or squeaking. Spiral flooring nails are sometimes used in other applications, such as installing tongue-and-groove paneling on ceilings.

- Galvanized nails, that have a zinc coating that resists rusting. They are used for outdoor projects.

- Wallboard nails, once the standard fastener for wallboard, are less common today because of the development of Phillips-head wallboard screws that drive quickly with a screw gun or drill and offer superior holding power.

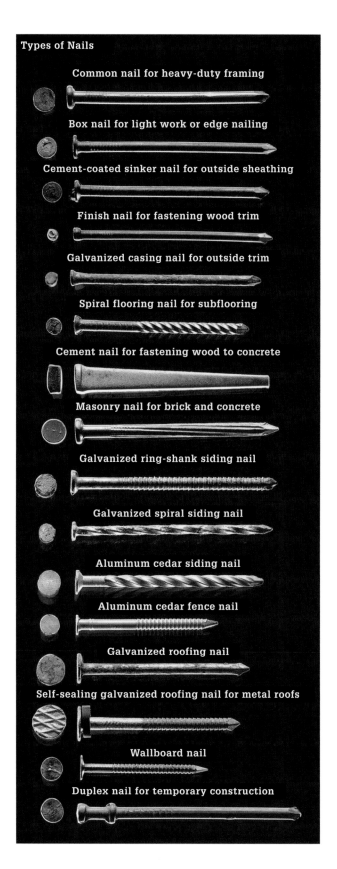

Types of Nails

Common nail for heavy-duty framing

Box nail for light work or edge nailing

Cement-coated sinker nail for outside sheathing

Finish nail for fastening wood trim

Galvanized casing nail for outside trim

Spiral flooring nail for subflooring

Cement nail for fastening wood to concrete

Masonry nail for brick and concrete

Galvanized ring-shank siding nail

Galvanized spiral siding nail

Aluminum cedar siding nail

Aluminum cedar fence nail

Galvanized roofing nail

Self-sealing galvanized roofing nail for metal roofs

Wallboard nail

Duplex nail for temporary construction

Nail Sizes ▶

The pennyweight scale that manufacturers use to size nails was developed centuries ago as an approximation of the number of pennies it would take to buy 100 nails of that size. The range of nail types available today (and what they cost) is much wider, but the scale is still in use.

Each pennyweight refers to a specific length (see chart, below), although you will find slight variations in length from one nail type to the next. For example, box nails of a given pennyweight are roughly ⅛" shorter than common nails of the same weight.

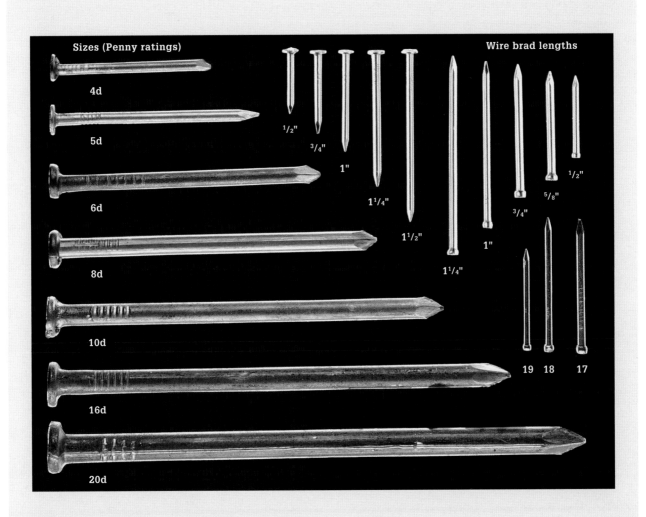

Estimating Nail Quantities

Estimate the number of nails you'll need for a project, then use the chart to determine approximately how many pounds of nails to purchase.

Note: Sizes and quantities not listed are less common, although they may be available through some manufacturers.

	Pennyweight	2d	3d	4d	5d	6d	7d	8d	10d	12d	16d	20d
	Length (in.)	1	1¼	1½	1⅝	2	2⅛	2½	3	3¼	3½	4
Nails per lb.	Common	870	543	294	254	167		101	66	61	47	29
	Box	635	473	406	236	210	145	94	88	71	39	
	Cement-Coated			527	387	293	223	153	111	81	64	52
	Finish	1350	880	630	535	288		196	124	113	93	39
	Masonry			155	138	100	78	64	48	43	34	

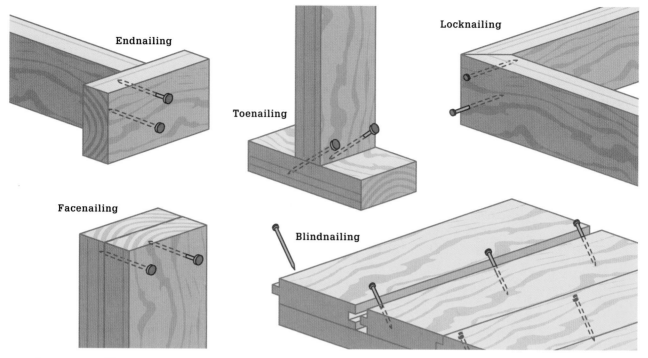

Use the proper nailing technique for the task. Endnailing is used to attach perpendicular boards when moderate strength is required. Toenail at a 45° angle for extra strength when joining perpendicular framing members. Facenail to create strong headers for door and window openings. Blindnail tongue-and-groove boards to conceal nails, eliminating the need to set nails and cover them with putty before painting or staining. Locknail outside miter joints in trim projects to prevent gaps from developing as the trim pieces dry.

Using Adhesives & Glues

Strengthen floors and decks and reduce squeaks with joist and deck adhesive. For outdoor applications, make sure you choose a waterproof adhesive.

Construction adhesive adds strength to carpentry and woodworking joints. It also has two advantages over glue. It has high initial tack, so parts don't slide apart, and it retains some flexibility after drying.

How to Use a Combination Square

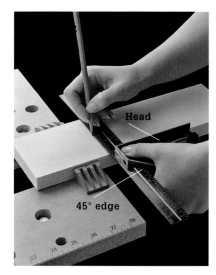

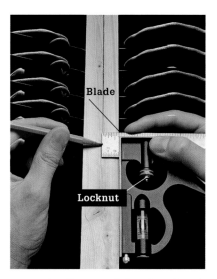

To mark a board for crosscutting, hold the square against the edge of the workpiece with the head locked, then use the edge of the blade to guide your pencil. Use the handle's 45° edge to mark boards for miter cuts.

To mark a line parallel to the edge of a board, lock the blade at the desired measurement, then hold the tip of the pencil along the end of the blade as you slide the tool along the workpiece. This is useful when marking reveal lines on window and door jambs.

To check for square, set the blade of a square flush with the end of the workpiece and set the head flush with one edge. If the end is a true 90°, there will not be a gap between the blade and the workpiece.

How to Use a Rafter Square

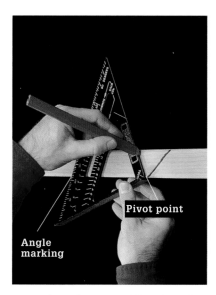

To mark angle cuts, position the rafter square's pivot point against the edge of the workpiece, and set the tool so the desired angle marking is aligned with the same edge. Scribe a line to mark the angle on the workpiece. Flip the tool over to mark angles in the opposite direction.

To mark crosscuts, place a rafter square's raised edge flush with one edge of the board, and use the perpendicular edge to guide your pencil. On wide boards, you'll need to flip the square to the board's other edge to extend the line across the board.

To guide a circular saw when making crosscuts, first align the blade of the saw with your cutting line. As you cut, hold the raised edge of the square against the front edge of the workpiece and the perpendicular edge flush with the foot of the saw.

Concrete

Use concrete to make solid footings that will support the weight of the deck. Concrete for footings is made from a mixture of portland cement, sand, and coarse gravel (¼ to 1½" in diameter). You can buy bags containing these dry materials premixed at building centers. For larger amounts, buy ready-mixed concrete in trailer loads that you can haul to the job site or, for very large amounts, consider ordering ready-mixed material from a concrete company that will deliver it (see opposite page).

For most deck projects, mixing your own concrete is easy and inexpensive. Combine premixed bags with water following the manufacturer's instructions in a wheelbarrow or with a power mixer, available at rental centers. Never use a partial bag of dry premixed concrete because the contents aren't evenly distributed throughout the bag.

The estimation charts below give approximate volumes of concrete. You may have a small amount of concrete left over after pouring footings or stair pads.

Pre-cast concrete footing piers are available at building centers for use where local Building Codes don't require poured footings. They are particularly useful on low-profile decks because joists can be placed directly in the grooves formed in the pier tops. Piers should be placed on a layer of compactible gravel. When the piers are used to support posts, use post anchors bolted to the piers.

Amount of Concrete Needed (cubic feet) ▶

No. of 8" Dia. Footings	Depth of Footings (feet)			
	1	2	3	4
2	¾	1½	2¼	3
3	1	2¼	3½	4½
4	1½	3	4½	6
5	2	3¾	5¾	7½
No. of 12" Dia. Footings	Depth of Footings (feet)			
	1	2	3	4
2	1½	3	4¾	6¼
3	2⅖	4¾	7	9½
4	3⅕	6	9½	12½
5	4	8	11¾	15¾

Pad Size	Cubic Feet
3 × 3' × 4" thick	3
3 × 4' × 4" thick	4
4 × 4' × 4" thick	5.4

Buying & Mixing Concrete

Buy premixed bags of dry concrete for small jobs.
A 60-lb. bag creates about ½ of a cubic foot of concrete.
A 90-lb. bag creates about ⅔ of a cubic foot.

Rent a power cement mixer for larger quantities of premixed bags. It blends 2 to 4 bags at a time (depending on the size of the mixer) quickly and thoroughly.

Buy ready-mixed concrete for larger jobs. Trailer loads are available at rental centers and are sold by the cubic yard. One cubic yard equals 27 cubic feet.

Buy ready-mixed concrete and have it delivered for projects requiring very large amounts. Many suppliers have pumps on their trucks so they can pour concrete directly into footings or pad locations, although they may charge extra for this service.

How to Dig & Pour Post Footings

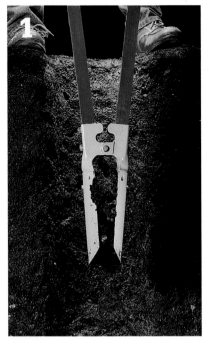

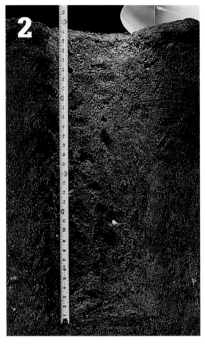

Dig holes for post footings with a clamshell digger or a power auger, centering the holes on the layout stakes. For holes deeper than 35", use a power auger.

Measure the hole depth. Local building codes specify the depth of footings. Cut away tree roots, if necessary, using a pruning saw.

Pour 2 to 3" of loose gravel in the bottom of each footing hole. Gravel will provide drainage under concrete footings.

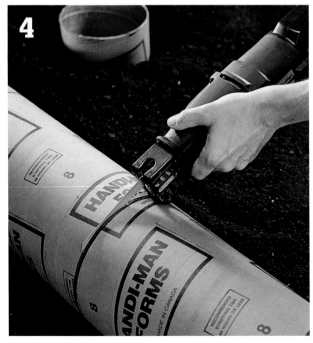

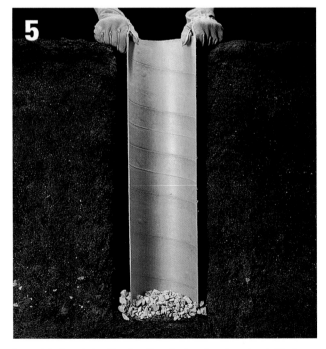

Add 2" to the hole depth so that the footings will be above ground level. Cut concrete tube forms to length, using a reciprocating saw or a handsaw. Make sure the cut is straight.

Insert tubes into the footing holes, leaving about 2" of tube above ground level. Use a level to make sure the tops of the tubes are level. Pack the soil around the tubes to hold them in place.

Mix dry ingredients for concrete in a wheelbarrow using a hoe.

Form a hollow in the center of the dry concrete mixture. Slowly pour a small amount of water into the hollow, and blend in the dry mixture with a hoe.

Add more water gradually, mixing thoroughly until the concrete is firm enough to hold its shape when sliced with a trowel.

Pour the concrete slowly into the tube form, guiding the concrete from the wheelbarrow with a shovel. Fill about half of the form using a long stick to tamp the concrete, filling any air gaps in the footing. Then finish pouring and tamping concrete into the form.

Level the concrete by pulling a 2 × 4 across the top of the tube form using a sawing motion. Add concrete to any low spots. Retie the mason's strings on the batterboards, and recheck the measurements.

(continued)

Insert a J-bolt at an angle into the wet concrete at the center of the footing.

Lower the J-bolt slowly into the concrete, wiggling it slightly to eliminate any air gaps.

Set the J-bolt so ¾ to 1" is exposed above the concrete. Brush away any wet concrete on the bolt threads with an old toothbrush.

Use a plumb bob to make sure the J-bolt is positioned exactly at the center of the post location.

Use a torpedo level to make sure the J-bolt is plumb. If necessary, adjust the bolt and repack the concrete. Let the concrete cure, then cut away the exposed portion of the tube with a utility knife.

How to Install Anchor Bolts with Epoxy

After the concrete footing has cured at least 48 hours and the bolt locations have been determined, drill a hole for the threaded rod using a hammer drill and a masonry bit sized to match the diameter of the rod. Make the vertical holes using a speed square to align the drill. Set the depth gauge of the drill so that ¾ to 1" of the rod will protrude above the footing surface.

Use a shop vacuum to remove the drilling debris. Clean the hole thoroughly using a long, thin object, such as a narrow blade screwdriver, to loosen the debris. If the surface isn't clean, the epoxy won't bond firmly with the concrete. Testfit the threaded rod to make certain it will insert to the proper depth.

Wrap masking tape around the top ¾ to 1" of the threaded rod. This will help you insert it to the proper depth and protect the threads from epoxy. Inject epoxy into the hole using the mixing syringe provided by the manufacturer. Use enough epoxy so a small amount is forced from the hole when the rod is fully inserted. Push the rod into the hole with a twisting motion as soon as the epoxy is injected because it begins to harden immediately.

Make certain the threaded rod is fully inserted, checking the height of the rod above the footing surface. Let the epoxy cure for 16 to 24 hours (follow the manufacturer's instructions). Curing times are affected by moisture and temperature.

If you can't push the rod in far enough, don't try pulling it out. Wait until the epoxy cures, then install a nut on the rod past the point where you need to cut it. Using a hacksaw or reciprocating saw with a metal cutting blade, trim it to the proper length above the footing surface. Remove the nut to rethread the cut end.

Determining Lumber Size

A deck has seven major structural parts: the ledger, decking, joists, one or more beams, posts, stairway stringers, and stairway treads. To create a working design plan and choose the correct lumber size, you must know the span limits of each part of the deck. The ledger is attached directly to the house and does not have a span limit.

A span limit is the safe distance a board can cross without support from underneath. The maximum safe span depends on the size and wood species of the board. For example, 2 × 6 southern pine joists spaced 16" on-center can safely span 9'9", while 2 × 10 joists can span 16'1".

Begin planning by first choosing the size and pattern for the decking. Use the tables on the opposite page. Then determine the size and layout of the joists and beams using the information on pages 230 to 232. In general, a deck designed with larger-size lumber, like 2 × 12 joists and beams, requires fewer pieces because the boards have a large span limit. Next, compute the correct size for the posts using the table on the opposite page. Finally, choose the stair and railing lumber that fits your plan, again using the tables on the opposite page.

Use the design plans to make a complete list of the quantities of each lumber size your deck requires. Add 10 percent to compensate for lumber flaws and construction errors. Full-service lumberyards have a fine lumber selection, but prices may be higher than those at home improvement centers. The quality of lumber at home centers can vary, so inspect the wood and handpick the pieces you want or add a larger percentage to compensate for lumber flaws. Both lumberyards and home centers will deliver lumber for a small fee and you can usually return unused, uncut lumber if you keep your receipts.

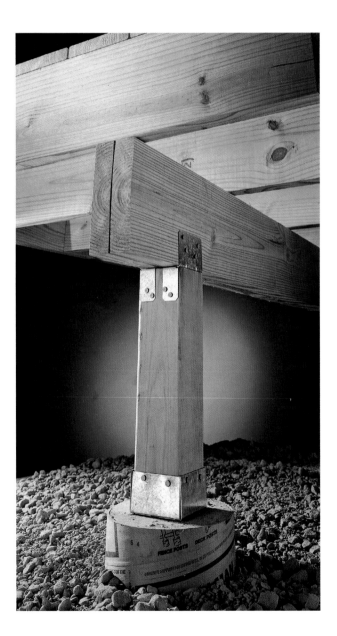

Nominal vs. Actual Lumber Dimensions ▶

Nominal	Actual
1 × 4	¾ × 3¾"
1 × 6	¾ × 5¾"
2 × 4	1½ × 3½"
2 × 6	1½ × 5½"
2 × 8	1½ × 7¼"
2 × 10	1½ × 9¼"
2 × 12	1½ × 11¼"
4 × 4	3½ × 3½"
6 × 6	5½ × 5½"

When planning a deck, remember that the actual size of lumber is smaller than the nominal size by which lumber is sold. Use the actual dimensions when drawing a deck design plan.

Lumber Grading Chart ▸

Much of today's lumber is still fairly wet when it is sold, so it's hard to predict how it will behave as it dries. But a quick inspection of each board at the lumberyard or home center will help you disqualify flawed boards. Lumber that is cupped, twisted, or crooked should not be used at full length. However, you may be able to cut out good sections for use as blocking or other short framing pieces. If a board is slightly bowed, you can probably flatten it out as you nail it. Checks, wanes, and knots are cosmetic flaws that seldom affect the strength of the board. The exception is a knot that is loose or missing. In this case, cut off the damaged area. Sections with splits should also be cut off. Splits are likely to spread as the wood dries.

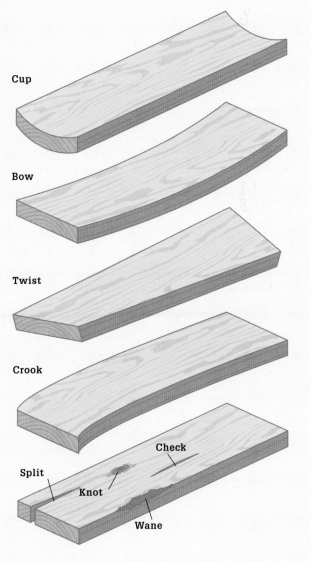

Grade stamps provide valuable information about a piece of lumber. The lumber's grade is usually indicated by the largest number stamped on the wood. Also stamped on each piece of lumber are its moisture content, species, and lumber mill of origin.

Grade	Description, uses
Clear	Free of knots and defects.
SEL STR or Select Structural	Good appearance, strength, and stiffness.
1,2,3	1,2,3 grades indicate knot size.
CONST or Construction	Both grades used for general framing.
STAND or Standard	Good strength and serviceability.
STUD or Stud	Special designation used in any stud application, including load-bearing walls.
UTIL or Utility	Economical choice for blocking and bracing.

Selecting the Right Lumber for a Project ▸

Picking the right wood for a project is a decision that will affect the durability and attractiveness of the final product. Some woods are more prone to warping than others, some are more resistant to decay, and some are superior when it comes to accepting a coat of paint. Matching styles and wood varieties will help to create a common theme throughout your home.

Lumber sizes, such as 2 × 4, are nominal dimensions, not actual dimensions. The actual size of the lumber is slightly smaller than the nominal size. When it is originally milled, lumber is cut at the nominal size; however, the boards are then planed down for a smoother finish, producing the actual dimensions you buy in the store.

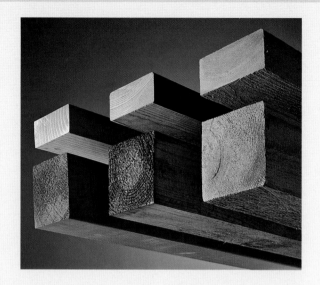

Softwood	Description	Uses
Cedar	Easy to cut, holds paint well. Heartwood resists decay.	Decks, shakes, shingles, posts, and other decay-prone surfaces.
Fir, larch	Stiff, hard wood. Holds nails well. Some varieties are hard to cut.	Framing materials, flooring, and subflooring.
Pine	Lightweight, soft wood with a tendency to shrink. Holds nails well. Some varieties resist decay.	Paneling, trim, siding, and decks.
Redwood	Lightweight, soft wood that holds paint well. Easy to cut. Heartwood resists decay and insect damage.	Outdoor applications, such as decks, posts, and fences.
Treated lumber	Chemically treated to resist decay. Use corrosion-resistant fasteners only. Wear protective eye wear and clothing to avoid skin, lung, and eye irritation.	Ground-contact and other outdoor applications where resistance to decay is important.

Hardwood	Description	Uses
Birch	Hard, strong wood that is easy to cut and holds paint well.	Painted cabinets, trim, and plywood.
Maple	Heavy, hard, strong wood that is difficult to cut with hand tools.	Flooring, furniture, and countertops.
Poplar	Soft, light wood that is easy to cut with hand or power tools.	Painted cabinets, trim, tongue-and-groove paneling, and plywood cores.
Oak	Heavy, hard, strong wood that is difficult to cut with hand tools.	Furniture, flooring, doors, and trim.
Walnut	Heavy, hard, strong wood that is easy to cut.	Fine woodwork, paneling, and mantelpieces.

Type	Description	Common Nominal Sizes	Actual Sizes
Dimensional lumber 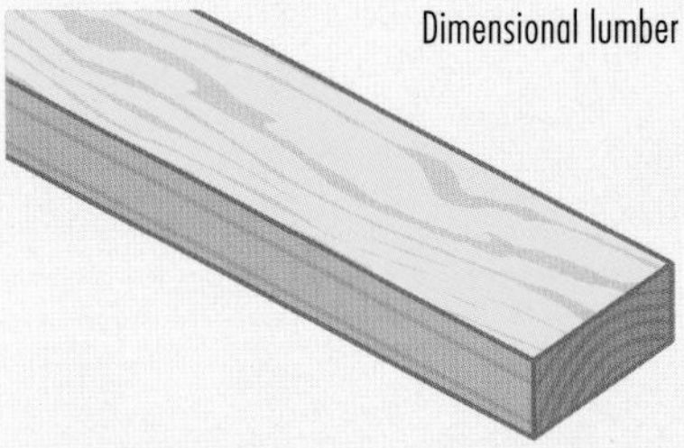	Used in framing of walls, ceilings, floors, and rafters, structural finishing, exterior decking, fencing, and stairs.	1 × 4 1 × 6 1 × 8 2 × 2 2 × 4 2 × 6 2 × 8	¾ × 3½" ¾ × 5½" ¾ × 7¼" 1½ × 1½" 1½ × 3½" 1½ × 5½" 1½ × 7¼"
Furring strips 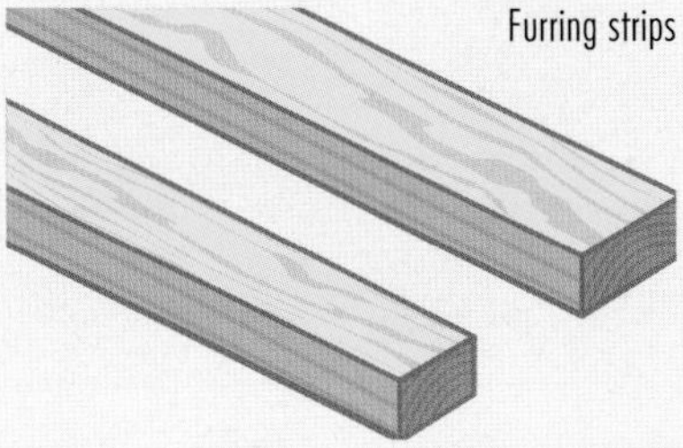	Used in framing of walls, ceilings, floors, and rafters, structural finishing, exterior decking, fencing, and stairs.	1 × 2 1 × 3	¾ × 1½" ¾ × 2½"
Tongue-and-groove paneling 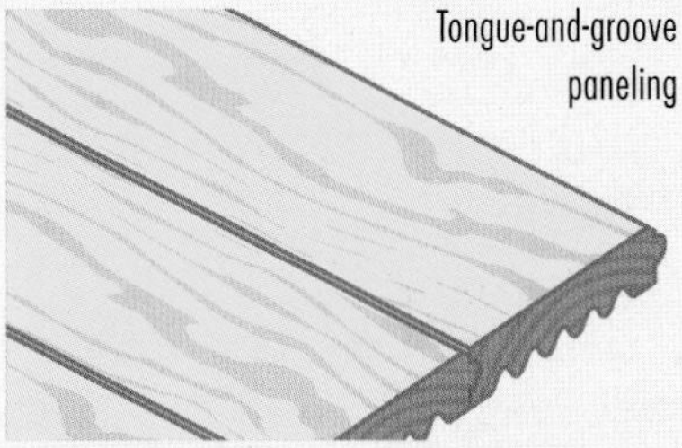	Used in wainscoting and full-length paneling of walls and ceilings.	5/16 × 4 1 × 4 1 × 6 1 × 8	Varies depending on milling process and application.
Finished boards 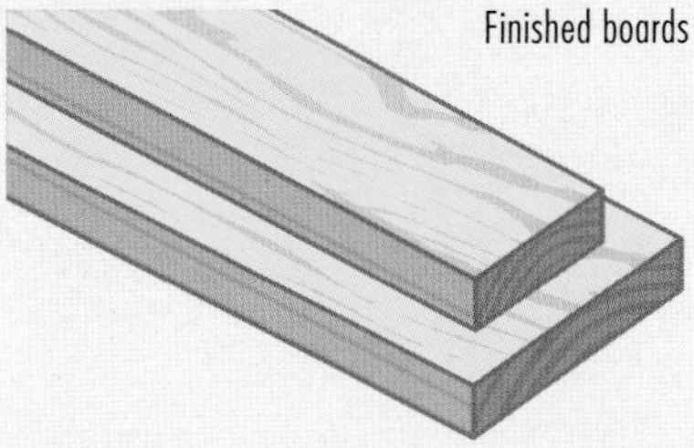	Used in trim, shelving, cabinetry, and other applications where a fine finish is required.	1 × 4 1 × 6 1 × 8 1 × 10 1 × 12	¾ × 3½" ¾ × 5½" ¾ × 7½" ¾ × 9½" ¾ × 11½"
Glue laminate 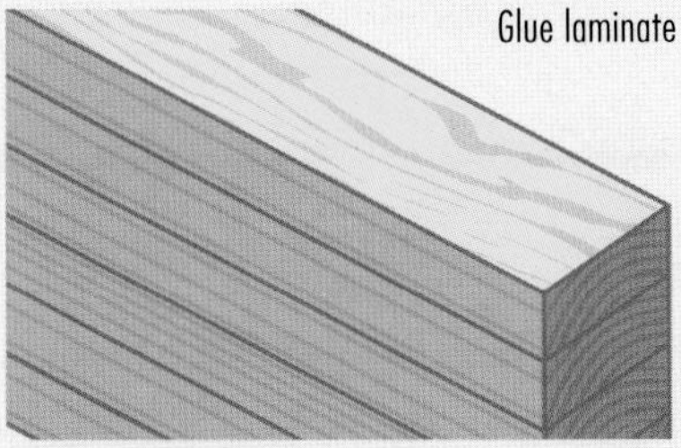	Composed of layers of lumber laminated to form a solid piece. Used for beams and joists.	4 × 10 4 × 12 6 × 10 6 × 12	3½ × 9 3½ × 12 3½ × 9 3½ × 12
Micro-lam 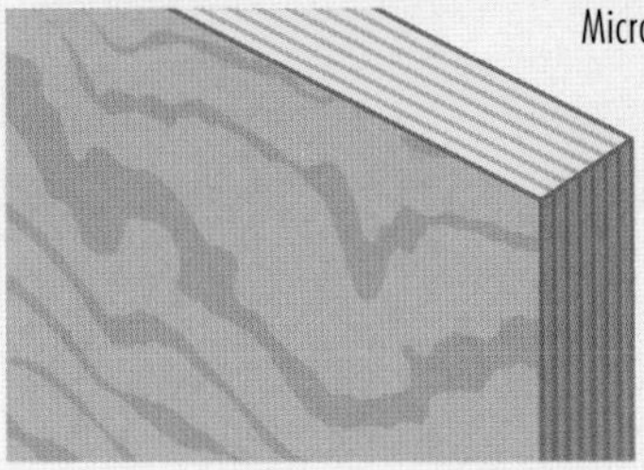	Composed of thin layers glued together for use in joists and beams.	4 × 12	3½ × 11⅞"

Conversion Charts

Metric Conversions

To Convert:	To:	Multiply by:
Inches	Millimeters	25.4
Inches	Centimeters	2.54
Feet	Meters	0.305
Yards	Meters	0.914
Square inches	Square centimeters	6.45
Square feet	Square meters	0.093
Square yards	Square meters	0.836
Ounces	Milliliters	30.0
Pints (U.S.)	Liters	0.473 (Imp. 0.568)
Quarts (U.S.)	Liters	0.946 (Imp. 1.136)
Gallons (U.S.)	Liters	3.785 (Imp. 4.546)
Ounces	Grams	28.4
Pounds	Kilograms	0.454

To Convert:	To:	Multiply by:
Millimeters	Inches	0.039
Centimeters	Inches	0.394
Meters	Feet	3.28
Meters	Yards	1.09
Square centimeters	Square inches	0.155
Square meters	Square feet	10.8
Square meters	Square yards	1.2
Milliliters	Ounces	.033
Liters	Pints (U.S.)	2.114 (Imp. 1.76)
Liters	Quarts (U.S.)	1.057 (Imp. 0.88)
Liters	Gallons (U.S.)	0.264 (Imp. 0.22)
Grams	Ounces	0.035
Kilograms	Pounds	2.2

Converting Temperatures

Convert degrees Fahrenheit (F) to degrees Celsius (C) by following this simple formula: Subtract 32 from the Fahrenheit temperature reading. Then, multiply that number by $\frac{5}{9}$. For example, 77°F - 32 = 45. 45 × $\frac{5}{9}$ = 25°C.

To convert degrees Celsius to degrees Fahrenheit, multiply the Celsius temperature reading by $\frac{9}{5}$. Then, add 32. For example, 25°C × $\frac{9}{5}$ = 45. 45 + 32 = 77°F.

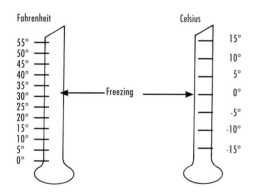

Metric Plywood Panels

Metric plywood panels are commonly available in two sizes: 1,200 mm × 2,400 mm and 1,220 mm × 2,400 mm, which is roughly equivalent to a 4 × 8-ft. sheet. Standard and Select sheathing panels come in standard thicknesses, while Sanded grade panels are available in special thicknesses.

Standard Sheathing Grade		Sanded Grade	
7.5 mm	($\frac{5}{16}$ in.)	6 mm	($\frac{4}{17}$ in.)
9.5 mm	($\frac{3}{8}$ in.)	8 mm	($\frac{5}{16}$ in.)
12.5 mm	($\frac{1}{2}$ in.)	11 mm	($\frac{7}{16}$ in.)
15.5 mm	($\frac{5}{8}$ in.)	14 mm	($\frac{9}{16}$ in.)
18.5 mm	($\frac{3}{4}$ in.)	17 mm	($\frac{2}{3}$ in.)
20.5 mm	($\frac{13}{16}$ in.)	19 mm	($\frac{3}{4}$ in.)
22.5 mm	($\frac{7}{8}$ in.)	21 mm	($\frac{13}{16}$ in.)
25.5 mm	(1 in.)	24 mm	($\frac{15}{16}$ in.)

Lumber Dimensions

Nominal - U.S.	Actual - U.S. (in inches)	Metric
1 × 2	$\frac{3}{4}$ × 1$\frac{1}{2}$	19 × 38 mm
1 × 3	$\frac{3}{4}$ × 2$\frac{1}{2}$	19 × 64 mm
1 × 4	$\frac{3}{4}$ × 3$\frac{1}{2}$	19 × 89 mm
1 × 5	$\frac{3}{4}$ × 4$\frac{1}{2}$	19 × 114 mm
1 × 6	$\frac{3}{4}$ × 5$\frac{1}{2}$	19 × 140 mm
1 × 7	$\frac{3}{4}$ × 6$\frac{1}{4}$	19 × 159 mm
1 × 8	$\frac{3}{4}$ × 7$\frac{1}{4}$	19 × 184 mm
1 × 10	$\frac{3}{4}$ × 9$\frac{1}{4}$	19 × 235 mm
1 × 12	$\frac{3}{4}$ × 11$\frac{1}{4}$	19 × 286 mm
1$\frac{1}{4}$ × 4	1 × 3$\frac{1}{2}$	25 × 89 mm
1$\frac{1}{4}$ × 6	1 × 5$\frac{1}{2}$	25 × 140 mm
1$\frac{1}{4}$ × 8	1 × 7$\frac{1}{4}$	25 × 184 mm
1$\frac{1}{4}$ × 10	1 × 9$\frac{1}{4}$	25 × 235 mm
1$\frac{1}{4}$ × 12	1 × 11$\frac{1}{4}$	25 × 286 mm
1$\frac{1}{2}$ × 4	1$\frac{1}{4}$ × 3$\frac{1}{2}$	32 × 89 mm
1$\frac{1}{2}$ × 6	1$\frac{1}{4}$ × 5$\frac{1}{2}$	32 × 140 mm
1$\frac{1}{2}$ × 8	1$\frac{1}{4}$ × 7$\frac{1}{4}$	32 × 184 mm
1$\frac{1}{2}$ × 10	1$\frac{1}{4}$ × 9$\frac{1}{4}$	32 × 235 mm
1$\frac{1}{2}$ × 12	1$\frac{1}{4}$ × 11$\frac{1}{4}$	32 × 286 mm
2 × 4	1$\frac{1}{2}$ × 3$\frac{1}{2}$	38 × 89 mm
2 × 6	1$\frac{1}{2}$ × 5$\frac{1}{2}$	38 × 140 mm
2 × 8	1$\frac{1}{2}$ × 7$\frac{1}{4}$	38 × 184 mm
2 × 10	1$\frac{1}{2}$ × 9$\frac{1}{4}$	38 × 235 mm
2 × 12	1$\frac{1}{2}$ × 11$\frac{1}{4}$	38 × 286 mm
3 × 6	2$\frac{1}{2}$ × 5$\frac{1}{2}$	64 × 140 mm
4 × 4	3$\frac{1}{2}$ × 3$\frac{1}{2}$	89 × 89 mm
4 × 6	3$\frac{1}{2}$ × 5$\frac{1}{2}$	89 × 140 mm

Liquid Measurement Equivalents

1 Pint	= 16 Fluid Ounces	= 2 Cups
1 Quart	= 32 Fluid Ounces	= 2 Pints
1 Gallon	= 128 Fluid Ounces	= 4 Quarts

Drill Bit Guide

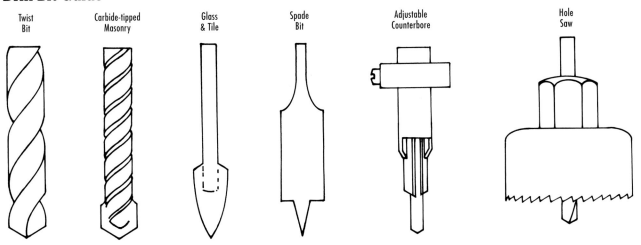

Twist Bit   Carbide-tipped Masonry   Glass & Tile   Spade Bit   Adjustable Counterbore   Hole Saw

Nails

Nail lengths are identified by numbers from 4 to 60 followed by the letter "d," which stands for "penny." For general framing and repair work, use common or box nails. Common nails are best suited to framing work where strength is important. Box nails are smaller in diameter than common nails, which makes them easier to drive and less likely to split wood. Use box nails for light work and thin materials. Most common and box nails have a cement or vinyl coating that improves their holding power.

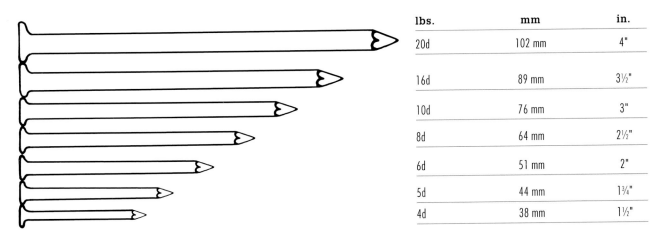

lbs.	mm	in.
20d	102 mm	4"
16d	89 mm	3½"
10d	76 mm	3"
8d	64 mm	2½"
6d	51 mm	2"
5d	44 mm	1¾"
4d	38 mm	1½"

Counterbore, Shank & Pilot Hole Diameters

Screw Size	Counterbore Diameter for Screw Head (in inches)	Clearance Hole for Screw Shank (in inches)	Pilot Hole Diameter	
			Hard Wood (in inches)	Soft Wood (in inches)
#1	.146 (9/64)	5/64	3/64	1/32
#2	1/4	3/32	3/64	1/32
#3	1/4	7/64	1/16	3/64
#4	1/4	1/8	1/16	3/64
#5	1/4	1/8	5/64	1/16
#6	5/16	9/64	3/32	5/64
#7	5/16	5/32	3/32	5/64
#8	3/8	11/64	1/8	3/32
#9	3/8	11/64	1/8	3/32
#10	3/8	3/16	1/8	7/64
#11	1/2	3/16	5/32	9/64
#12	1/2	7/32	9/64	1/8

Resources

Underdeck (p. 99)
Inter-joist ceiling system
877-805-7156
www.underdeck.com

ScreenTight (p. 108)
Porch screening systems, screen doors & accessories
800-768-7325
www.screentight.com

SunPorch Structures, Inc. (p. 182)
Sun porch and sunroom kits
800-221-2550
www.sunporch.com

Palram Americas (p. 120)
Suntuf ® corrugated polycarbonate building panels
and Palsun® flat extruded polycarbonate sheeting
800-999-9928
www.palramamericas.com

Sunrooms by Design, Inc. (p. 200)
Prefabricated sunroom kits (professional installation)
(952) 226-4540
www.minnesotasunroom.com

Sunspace (p. 200)
Maintenance free sunrooms
800-755-3365
www.sunspacesunrooms.com

Photography Credits

Alamy / www.alamy.com
p. 24 (lower)

Amdega, Ltd.
p. 28 (lower)

Distinctive Designs
p. 99 (lower)

Four Seasons Sunrooms
p. 170 (lower right)

Fritz Van der Schulenberg / The Interior Archive
p. 170 (top), 173

Istock / www.istockphoto.com
p. 4, 8, 9 (all), 11 (lower two), 12, 13 (top left & lower), 14, 16, 17, 18 (top), 19, 21 (top), 24 (top), 25 (top), 26 (top & lower right), 28, 29, 33 (lower left), 156, 180

Lindal Cedar Homes
p. 23 (lower), 168, 170 (lower left), 172

NFRC
p. 179

Jerry Pavia / Jerry Pavia Photography, Inc.
p. 6, 10 (lower), 11 (top), 18 (lower), 21 (lower), 23 (top)

Beth Singer / www.bethsingerphotographer.com
p. 13 (top right)

Ray Strawbridge / www. strawbridgephoto.com
p. 20

Sunporch Structures, Inc.
p. 22, 25 (lower), 27, 174, 175, 184 (all)

Contacts

Amdega, Ltd.
Conservatories
www.amdega.co.uk

Distinctive Designs
www.distinctivedesigns4you.com
423-505-7457

Four Seasons Sunrooms
www.fourseasonssunrooms.com
800-368-7732

Lindal Cedar Homes
www.lindal.com
800-426-0536

NFRC (National Fenestration Rating Council)
www.efficientwindows.org
202-530-2254

Sunporch Structures, Inc.
www.sunporch.com
866-919-9620

Index

Also From **CREATIVE PUBLISHING international**

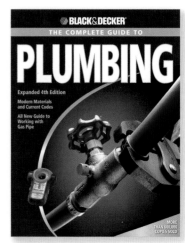

ISBN 1-58923-378-6

ISBN 1-58923-355-7

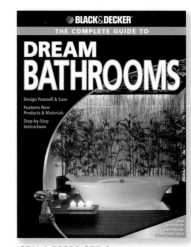

ISBN 1-58923-377-8

Creative Publishing
international

400 First Avenue North • Suite 300 • Minneapolis, MN 55401 • www.creativepub.com